PARTY EATS

PARTY EATS

DELICIOUS FOOD FROM EAST AND WEST

YAN-KIT SO
and
PAUL BLOOMFIELD

PIATKUS

© 1988 Yan-Kit So and Paul Bloomfield

First published in 1988 by
Judy Piatkus (Publishers) Limited,
5 Windmill Street, London W1P 1HF

British Library Cataloguing in Publication Data

So, Yan-Kit
    Party eats.
    1. Food: Dishes for buffets & dishes for
    supper parties – Recipes
    I. Title II. Bloomfield, Paul
    641.5′68
    ISBN 0–86188–781–6

Design by Sue Storey
Photography by James Murphy
Drawings by Paul Saunders

Typeset in Lasercomp Sabon
Printed and bound in Great Britain by
Butler & Tanner Ltd, Frome, Somerset

CONTENTS

INTRODUCTION
Yan-Kit So

Not many cocktail parties have a reincarnation in book form, but the one I gave in October 1987, to my surprise, sowed the seeds for this book. When I decided to give the party, I already had in mind a mixed menu of things Chinese and Western, believing that my guests should have the best of both worlds. I asked Paul Bloomfield, whose delicious finger-food had impressed me at a meeting of the Guild of Food Writers two years earlier, if his company, Nickleby's, would be prepared to serve Chinese eats at my party as well as their own Western food. He was keen, and so for three days he and his staff learned from and cooked with me in my kitchen, preparing a range of things Chinese that I was planning for the party.

The menu, as I recall, read like this:

Spinach and Smoked Salmon Roulades
Artichoke Hearts with Goat Cheese
Vegetarian Spring Rolls
Char-Siu Tartlets
Palate-Cleansing Mange-Tout
Braised Bamboo Shoots
Wriggling Prawns
Spicy Cucumber
Savoury Cashew Nuts

On the evening of the party I was busy receiving friends, and soon afterwards, or so it seemed, saying goodbye to them. Their parting remarks, so complimentary about the food, I at first took for granted as polite hyperbole until Gill Cormode, editor of my *Wok Cookbook* published by Piatkus, and Felicity Bryan, my literary agent, came over with whimsical smiles: 'We have a book for you. The food is so special that we want you to put it down in a book.' Could they simply be echoing the sentiments of the other guests? But they meant it.

When we got down to business, I proposed to my publisher that a book comprising my recipes and Paul Bloomfield's, a mix and match of East and West, would have the most to offer to all those wishing to give a cocktail party and serve eats that are distinctive rather than run-of-the-mill. When I broached the subject to Paul he was very enthusiastic, and thus we began the co-authorship of this book.

The concept of a cocktail party, in which people mill around with a glass in their hands savouring titbits and conversing with each other, is decidedly Western rather than Chinese. And yet, paradoxically, so much in the repertory of the Chinese cuisine lends itself naturally to cocktail party food. Substitute alcoholic drinks or wines for Chinese tea, and you will have the full spectrum of dimsums (Chinese hors d'oeuvres), steamed, fried or deep-fried, at your command to complement your drinks. Many stir-fried dishes, cut up into bite-sized pieces or lumps exuding mouth-watering fragrance, are also desirable cocktail party food. The only snag is that most stir-fries and dimsums, at their optimum served hot or crisp, necessitate an immediacy of action in the kitchen. No problem if the party is catered, but not ideal if you yourself have to stir-fry or deep-fry and also mingle with your guests. But most of us, when we give a party, do the sensible thing and bring in some help, either paid or drawn from friends or relations, so that the fun and burden of preparation – and any last minute panic – are shared.

In this book, even though I have derived inspiration from dimsum and stir-fries, I have left alone those recipes so taxing in time and skill as to be best enjoyed in a Chinese restaurant. Instead I have concentrated on practicable ones well within the realms of possibility at home. In some recipes, having benefited from a Western perspective through working with Paul, I have married certain aspects of Chinese cooking, whether ingredients or techniques, with those of other cuisines – and, I may add, to successful effect. There are some twelve Chinese recipes that involve deep-frying, but I make no apology for them. That deep-fried food, crisp to the bite and bursting with fragrance and flavour, is unrivalled with drinks and wines seems to be a universal truth. Not surprisingly, the Chinese have always served it with their wines which they warm up in an earthenware pot. The deep-frying itself, for which only vegetable oil is used, can be done in either a wok or a deep-fryer, a utensil many families already use to fry potato chips in.

You need not give a party in order to use this book. Choose at random one or two eats to serve with drinks before dinner, and you won't be disappointed; or use one of the recipes – maybe Skate Leaves, Half-Moon Wontons, Wriggling Prawns or Glazed Chicken – as a first course. As to how to pair the Chinese and Western recipes and what the ratio should be, again I say do as your fancy takes you. On page 15 Paul has some suggestions for you which all work well.

Enjoy the eats and have fun. I should like to dedicate this book to everyone who wishes to give a party.

Before handing over to Paul let me say a few words about one or two special techniques and some important Chinese ingredients which are available in Chinese shops and many good supermarkets.

Note: Yan-Kit's recipies from the East bear the Fish logo

SPECIAL CHINESE INGREDIENTS

Bamboo shoots
Young shoots of bamboo, cultivated in China for the table, give a contrast of texture when used with other ingredients. Fresh bamboo shoots are seldom if ever available in the West, so we have no option but to use the canned product which, fortunately, retains its crisp texture.

Dried Chinese black mushrooms
Known to many by the Japanese name shiitake, these cultivated tree fungi are black in colour and vary in size and thickness according to their quality. They lend flavour as well as absorb other tastes, which in turn make them even more succulent. They have to be reconstituted before use (see page 13).

Dried shrimps
Orangey pink in colour, their saltiness is mitigated by a savoury-sweet overtone. They are often used in stuffings.

Candy crystal sugar
Crystallised, pale topaz coloured cane sugar comes in lumps and has a 'pure' taste. It will keep indefinitely in a dry container. Demerara or white granulated sugar can be used as a substitute.

Chilli sauce
Usually bottled, this orange-red sauce is made of crushed fresh chilli peppers, vinegar, salt and plums. It varies in degree of fiery spiciness, depending on the brand and specific label, which may be marked 'sweet', 'hot' or even 'extra hot' – so watch out when using it! It is used both as a seasoning and as a dip for food.

Fresh bean curd (tofu)
Firm ivory-white curd made from ground soya beans and sold in cakes varying in size but commonly 1–1¼ inch (2.5–3 cm) thick and 2¼–2½ inches (6–6.5 cm) square. It is very healthy and nutritious, and is widely used in the Chinese cuisine. Tofu is its Japanese name.

Hoisin sauce
Lusciously reddish brown, made from soya beans, salt, wheat flour, sugar, vinegar, garlic, chilli and sesame oil and with a resultant savoury-sweet but tangy taste, this is used both as a seasoning and as a dipping sauce for meats such as roast duck and roast pork. It comes in bottles or cans.

Hot oil
Sometimes also labelled 'hot chilli oil' or 'chilly pepper oil', it is made by steeping dried red chilli flakes in heated oil and is sold in bottles.

Chinese rice vinegar
Clear vinegar made from rice, it is milder than white wine vinegar. Japanese rice vinegar is sweeter than Chinese rice vinegar.

Sesame oil
Thick, aromatic and light brown in colour, this oil is pressed from roasted white sesame seeds. It is quite different from the cold-pressed Middle Eastern sesame oil, which should not be used as a substitute. It is best sprinkled on food just before serving, although it can also be used for marinating ingredients. It keeps for a long time in a cool place.

Shaoxing wine
Amber-coloured Chinese wine made from glutinous rice, this is used both for drinking and for cooking. As a drink, it tastes much better warmed; for cooking, a medium-dry sherry can be used as a good substitute.

Sichuan peppercorns
Also known as *fagara*, these small, reddish brown peppercorns are a special product of Sichuan province in Western China. Not as burning hot as black peppercorns, they produce a slight numbing effect made more enticing by their aroma.

Soy sauce
Made from fermented, protein-rich soya beans, this is the indispensable seasoning in Chinese cooking. There are two main kinds, both of which are used in Chinese homes and restaurants: thick soy sauce is darker in colour, thicker in consistency and less salty in taste, while thin soy sauce is lighter,

and more salty. Often they are used together in conjunction with salt, but since thick soy sauce gives a reddish brown hue to food, do not use it for marinating or seasoning ingredients when a light appearance is called for. Soy sauce is usually packaged in bottles but also comes in cans. A very popular brand exported from China, Pearl River Bridge, labels its bottles of thin or light soy sauce 'superior soy', and its thick or dark 'soy, superior sauce' – with a telling '*épais*' 'fake' underneath.

Spring roll wrappers (skins)

Transparent like rice paper and about 8–10 inches (20–25 cm) square, the skins are made of wheat flour and sold frozen in packets. Once thawed, the wrappers are easily pulled apart. When using them, pull one out at a time and cover the rest in a plastic bag; otherwise, they dry out very quickly.

Star anise

The French use anise seeds in their cooking but the Chinese use the whole, eight-segmented hard spice, with its liquorice taste, to flavour their stews and braised dishes. Reddish brown in colour, it does resemble a star, hence its name.

Tangerine peel

The dark brown, hard and brittle peel of the tangerine, dried in the sun, is often used in conjunction with star anise and Sichuan peppercorns. Candied orange peels should *not* be used as a substitute.

White glutinous rice

More rounded in shape than long-grain rice, white glutinous rice is sticky when cooked.

Wonton skins (wrappers)

Made from wheat flour, egg and water, they are usually sold fresh in packets of 3 inch (7.5 cm) squares. They can be frozen.

White sesame seeds

Tiny, flat, white seeds from the sesame plant, these keep for a long time in a screw-top jar.

Water chestnuts
The fresh water chestnut is a corm of mahogany-brown colour grown in swampy ground in China. When peeled, it has a crisp texture and is often used in meat and fish dishes. For easy availability, we resort to the canned product in this book.

Yellow bean sauce
A brown purée of crushed and fermented yellow soya beans, wheat flour, salt and water, usually sold in cans or jars. Once opened, the sauce can be stored in the refrigerator for a long time.

Nori
Dark brown or deep green in colour, this Japanese seaweed comes in dried sheets of a standard size of about 8 × 7 inch (20 × 17.5 cm). It is sold in Japanese and some other Oriental shops, usually in packets of ten sheets. Once a packet is opened, keep the sheets out of sunlight in an airtight container.

Five-spice powder
A finely ground golden brown powder made up of five or six spices, including star anise, cinnamon, fennel, cloves and Sichuan peppercorns.

TECHNIQUES

How to reconstitute dried Chinese mushrooms

Pluck off the stalks with your fingers if you can do so without breaking up the mushrooms, and save them for the stockpot; alternatively, cut them off with a knife or scissors after the mushrooms have been reconstituted. To reconstitute the mushrooms, pour over them enough warm water to cover by $1\frac{1}{2}$ inch (4 cm) and leave to soak for about 30 minutes, or longer. Drain, leaving the mushrooms damp and saving the soaking liquid for the stockpot.

How to prepare spiced salt

Heat a dry wok or frying pan over medium heat until hot but not smoking. Add 2 tablespoons salt and stir continuously for about 5 minutes, or until very hot and slightly greyish in colour. Transfer to a small bowl, add 1 teaspoon five-spice powder and $\frac{1}{2}$ teaspoon ground white or black pepper, and mix well.

How to prepare cooked groundnut oil

Pour a small amount – up to 8 fl oz (250 ml) – of groundnut oil into a wok or a small saucepan and heat over a medium or high heat until the first sign of smoke appears. Immediately remove the wok from the heat, and let the oil cool before using it. The Chinese use it often on blanched vegetables or steamed dishes.

How to make ginger juice

Peel a large chunk of fresh ginger root, chop it very finely or grate it, then squeeze out the juice into a bowl, using your hand or a garlic press. Discard the pulp. The juice keeps for a long time if refrigerated; a small amount of Shaoxing wine or medium-dry sherry can also be added to the juice.

13

PREPARING *for a* PARTY

Paul Bloomfield

Parties should be fun for guests and hosts alike, and one of the aims of this book is to dispel any alarm you may feel when faced with the prospect of preparing for a party.

As a host, you want to spend as much time with your guests as possible. There can be nothing more frustrating than inviting people round and then not having time to talk to them – especially, as is often the case with parties, when you have not seen them for some time. You can go a long way towards avoiding this eventuality by preparing most of the food in advance. At the end of this introduction I suggest party menus which will enable you to do just that. Naturally, if you want to serve hot or warm food there will always be some last-minute cooking, but I have tried to maintain a balance to allow you to plan confidently ahead.

By selecting a balanced menu, you will help yourself to feel completely at ease and in control of your party. I always spend a lot of time at this planning stage. Do not choose an entire menu that needs to be finished off at the last minute, however. If you do, you will never be out of the kitchen, and your guests may have fairly long gaps between food! Nevertheless, not to include one or two items that require last-minute cooking would be to deny your guests a lot of enjoyment. Deep-fried things, for example, are always extremely popular and go amazingly well with drinks.

If you are holding a large party, I strongly recommend that you have an assistant or two. If you are married, do not choose your spouse. He or she would probably only get in the way, and would be much better employed greeting your guests and topping up glasses. You would be wiser to ask a favourite aunt, a friend or an outside helper. One thing is for certain – you will never regret having someone there to help.

Before the party, clear as many work surfaces as possible. Decide in advance what plates and dishes you will be using and have them ready, and do not imagine that you will have time to wash them up during the party and use them again. Also, choose two or three garnishes and have them to hand – you will need these if you are serving food that requires last-minute cooking. There is a trend, certainly among some caterers, to be over-ingenious with party food, but in this book, for the most part, we have advocated a more relaxed style of presentation, concentrating on flavour and originality.

Unusual serving dishes will do much to compliment the presentation. Choose stark coloured plates rather than painted or decorative ones as they show up the food better. Interesting shapes and scolloped edges are very effective, and large platters give a better overall effect than small round plates. Natural products always look good: use a wooden tray, or a bread board or a basket, or maybe a hollowed-out flat loaf of bread.

Start the party off with something easy that is ready the moment your guests arrive. Something cold, such as crudités with a couple of dips, is ideal. Move on to something hot, and after that alternate between hot and cold. During the party take note of what is most popular and regulate its distribution so that late-comers see the full extent of your repertoire. Finish on something warm or sweet – a sweet item often helps to convey the message that the party is over, which can be opportune.

Disasters ... well, everybody has these and only liars would deny that they do. 'Stay calm' appears to be the wisest maxim to apply when disasters occur. More immediately to the point, however, is to get rid of the evidence, since having it there for all to see may give an unnecessary battering to your confidence. If you have something in reserve that can be quickly made up into an emergency canapé, then set your assistant to this task – deep fried croûtes of bread with a spoonful of taramasalata or some cream cheese on top are fail-safe escapes. If this does not appear to be so easy, don't worry about it: one less item on the menu will not matter. No one will miss what they have not seen, and if they have seen it, just tell them it was so popular that it has all been eaten up by greedier guests.

Garnishes

In a catering situation, where large quantities of food are prepared everyday, 'garnish' usually means whatever is in the refrigerator that has colour and can be adapted to enhance a dish. This could be tiny, thin strips of red or yellow pepper, segments of fruit with the peel removed if necessary (remember that any garnish you use should be edible), perhaps strands of chive or the smallest sprigs of dill.

Finally, do not sniff too much at the commonplace chopped parsley: it has been the saviour of many a colourless, albeit delicious, canapé.

MENUS

Large cocktail party for 60 people

Fillet Steak with Stroganoff Dip
Sweet and Sour Wontons
Stuffed Chicken Wings
Tartlets of Jerusalem Artichoke Purée
Skate Leaves
Sweet Pepper Salad
Stuffed Baby Tomatoes
Miniature Pancakes
Fruit Fondue

Last-minute 'let's meet at my place
before we . . .' eats

Salsify
Smoked Lamb
Stuffed Lychees
Vegetable Tempura

Pre-dinner party nibbles

Sweet Potato Chips with Avocado
and Prawn Dip
Savoury Crispy Bean Curd
Crème Fraîche Piroshkis
Salmon Brochettes

Small drinks party for 15 people

Asparagus with Clam and Lime Sauce
Warm Oysters in Courgette Wells
Aromatic Quails' Eggs
Half-Moon Wontons
Stuffed Chicory Leaves
Wriggling Prawns

COLD
PARTY EATS

SMOKED SALMON PARCELS

Smoked salmon in any shape or form bespeaks the extravagant host, so this lavish combination will make your guests feel well and truly spoiled.

SERVES 10

INGREDIENTS

12 oz (350 g) thinly sliced smoked salmon
1 lb (450 g) smoked salmon pieces
½ pint (300 ml) double cream
freshly ground black pepper
7 fl oz (200 ml) fish stock
2 tablespoons powdered gelatine
juice of ½ lemon
juice and rind of 1 lime
16–20 fresh chives, each about 8 inches (20 cm) long
2 lemons, cut into thin wedges

1. Cut the sliced smoked salmon into approximately 4 inch (10 cm) squares and set aside. Put any trimmings into the bowl of a food processor with the smoked salmon pieces and mix to a paste. You will need to stop the motor half way through and scrape down the sides of the bowl. When the paste is smooth, transfer it to a mixing bowl.

2. Lightly whip the cream using a hand-held electric beater, and fold it into the smoked salmon paste. Season with black pepper, then return the mixture to the processor.

3. Measure the fish stock into a heatproof bowl and sprinkle on the gelatine. Leave to set for about 5 minutes.

4. Place the bowl of stock in a small saucepan containing about 1 inch (2.5 cm) of boiling water and stir over a gentle heat until the gelatine has dissolved. Remove the bowl from the heat, using a cloth to protect your hands.

5. Switch on the food processor and pour in the fish stock while the motor is running. This will ensure that the gelatine is thoroughly mixed throughout the mousse. Keeping the motor running, add the lemon juice, lime juice and lime rind. Switch off the processor and transfer the mousse to a shallow dish – a gratin dish or something similar. Cover with cling film and refrigerate for 1–2 hours, until set.

6. Assemble the smoked salmon parcels one at a time, returning the mousse to the refrigerator while you are working on each one. Scoop a teaspoon of mousse on to a smoked salmon square, then fold the edges of the square around the mousse as though wrapping a tiny gift. Place the parcel, with the join underneath, on a tray in the refrigerator while you prepare the remaining parcels. When all the parcels are wrapped, leave them in the refrigerator for 30 minutes so that they will be chilled into shape.

7. Tie up each parcel with a strand of chive. If you do not have enough length in the chive strand, split it down the centre for three-quarters of its length and tie up the parcel with the untidy end of the chive underneath. Serve one or perhaps two parcels per guest, accompanied by lemon wedges to squeeze over the parcels.

PHYLLO PASTRY TULIPS

INGREDIENTS

12 oz (350 g) sliced smoked
    halibut
¾ pint (450 ml) double cream,
    lightly whipped
freshly ground black pepper
6 fl oz (175 ml) fish stock
2 tablespoons powdered gelatine
juice of 1 lime
12 sheets phyllo pastry
2 oz (50 g) butter, melted
slivers of sweet red and yellow
    pepper, for decoration

A caterer can judge the success of a canapé by the speed at which it disappears, and we find that this idea has great appeal. The smoky nip of the mousse and the dryness of the phyllo are an excellent accompaniment to champagne. There is such an abundance and variety of good smoked fish available that you can adapt this simple recipe to create your own versions.

SERVES 15

1. Put the smoked halibut in a food processor and mix to a coarse paste. Make sure that all the halibut is evenly blended. Fold the cream into the halibut paste and season with black pepper.

2. Measure the stock into a heatproof bowl and sprinkle on the gelatine. Leave to set for 5 minutes. Stand the bowl in a saucepan containing about 1 inch (2.5 cm) of boiling water and stir over gentle heat until the gelatine has dissolved – this will take about 3 minutes.

3. Slowly pour the gelatine mixture into the food processor with the halibut, with the motor running. Add the lime juice and continue to blend until all the ingredients are incorporated, then switch off the processor. Pour the mixture into a shallow dish and refrigerate for about an hour, until set.

4. Cut the phyllo pastry sheets into 2 inch (5 cm) squares. Cover and refrigerate until ready to use, to prevent the pastry from drying out.

5. Heat the oven to 400°F/200°C/gas mark 6 and butter about 36 small tartlet moulds. Use either individual moulds or sheets of moulds – you will find sheets of moulds much the easier. Take a phyllo square and brush one side with melted butter. Butter two more squares in the same way and place the three squares unevenly in a tartlet mould so that their corners resemble the petals of a tulip. Make more tulips with the remaining phyllo pastry. Bake the phyllo tulips for 2–3 minutes, until lightly browned, then remove from the oven and leave to cool.

6. Remove the mousse from the refrigerator. Take a cup of hot water and a teaspoon and, dipping the spoon into the hot water

first, scoop a small oval-shaped mound of mousse into each tulip. Decorate the filled tulips with slivers of red and yellow pepper.

7. Refrigerate the phyllo tulips until you are ready to serve them – they will keep in this finished form for 2–3 hours. Do not attempt to cover them during this time as they are very delicate.

Note: A quicker alternative to the halibut mousse would be a warm curried prawn mixture. The unfilled phyllo tulips may be kept overnight in the refrigerator without deteriorating, as long as you remember that they are extremely fragile.

SPINACH *and* SMOKED SALMON ROULADES

INGREDIENTS

6 oz (150 g) frozen finely chopped
  spinach
½ oz (15 g) butter
small pinch grated nutmeg
freshly ground black pepper
6 large eggs, separated
4 oz (100 g) cream cheese
1–2 teaspoons freshly squeezed
  lemon juice
6 oz (175 g) thinly sliced smoked
  salmon, cut into thin strips

These tiny roulades are an excellent idea for larger numbers and you can produce a lot in a short space of time. They can also be made a day in advance. The fillings can be varied to contrast and complement each other – for example, some strips of smoked halibut or smoked venison would be equally delicious. Serve a mixture of different fillings on the same plate.

SERVES 20–25

1. Heat the oven to 375°F/190°C/gas mark 5 and line the base of a shallow baking tin, about 14 × 10 × 2 inches (35 × 25 × 5 cm), with cling film.

2. Put the spinach in a heavy-bottomed saucepan and add the butter, nutmeg, and some black pepper. Set the pan over a medium heat, shaking it until the excess moisture in the spinach has evaporated – this will take about 4 minutes.

3. Transfer the spinach to a mixing bowl. Allow to cool for about 5 minutes then add the egg yolks. Lightly beat the ingredients together.

4. Beat the egg whites until they form stiff peaks, then add them to the bowl and fold in well. Pour the egg and spinach mixture into the prepared baking tin, spreading it evenly over the base with a spatula.

5. Bake the roulade in the oven for 10–12 minutes. As soon as it is firm enough to peel away from the cling film, remove it from the oven. Lay the roulade on a flat surface to cool.

6. Blend the cream cheese to a spreading consistency with lemon juice, making sure it is not too runny. Cut the cooled roulade into quarters and spread them with cream cheese, then lay strips of smoked salmon on top, parallel with a long edge of the roulade – if you use thin strips of smoked salmon you will get a neater roll. Beginning at a long edge, roll up the roulades quite tightly, then wrap them in foil. Refrigerate for at least an hour (they can be left for up to 24 hours).

7. When ready to serve, unwrap the roulades and discard the foil. Trim off the untidy edges and cut each roulade into 12–15 slices. Serve very cold.

Note: This recipe can be easily adapted to make a vegetarian roulade – simply substitute sweet red pepper strips for the smoked salmon. The end result is delicious, colourful and also a great deal less expensive! The peppers should be seeded, cut into thin strips and blanched in boiling water for 2 minutes, then drained and allowed to cool before being rolled up in the roulades.

Alternatively, to improve the flavour even more, the peppers could be charred under a hot grill, and the skins stripped off before slicing (see page 52 for this method).

SKATE LEAVES

INGREDIENTS

2¼–2½ lb (1–1.2 kg) skate wings, rinsed

¼ pint (150 ml) olive oil

1–1½ inch (2.5–3.5 cm) piece fresh ginger root, peeled and finely shredded

10 large spring onions, trimmed, cut into 1 inch (2.5 cm) sections and finely shredded

3 tablespoons thin or light soy sauce

2 tablespoons sesame oil

freshly ground black or white pepper

2 heads iceberg lettuce

The mashed skate provides a delectable contrast to the crunchy iceberg, a lettuce more valued for its texture than its taste. Olive oil is used not just because of the flavour it adds to the skate but also because, being monounsaturated, one can use it freely with a clear conscience to produce the desired effect.

If skate is not available, or if you should prefer another fish, you could use haddock or hake. They are both good. Cod and plaice are less preferable; the former is rather chewy and the latter somewhat tasteless.

SERVES 20

1. Lay the skate wings on a heatproof dish with raised edges and place it in a steamer. Steam (see Note below), covered, over a high heat for about 20 minutes, or until well done, the flesh coming away from the bones easily.

2. Remove the dish from the steamer. Using either chopsticks or a fork and spoon, remove the flesh from the bones and put it in a bowl. Discard the bones, skin and the liquid in the dish.

3. Heat a wok over a high heat until smoke rises. Pour in the olive oil, swirl it around, and heat until smoke rises again. Add the ginger, stir a few times, then add the spring onions and continue to stir for about 30 seconds to release the aroma. Add the fish, and turn and toss for 2–3 minutes. The fish will disintegrate. Reduce the heat, add the soy sauce, and stir and mix for another 5–10 minutes, turning over the mashed fish as well so that it does not stick to the bottom of the wok. Add the sesame oil and stir for another 2 minutes. By now, any excess moisture from the fish should have been absorbed, but the fish should still be moist. Scoop the contents of the wok on to a dish and allow to cool. Season with some pepper.

4. Meanwhile, prepare the leaves. Using a pair of scissors, cut the lettuce leaves into about 50 squares or rectangular pieces, with sides measuring 4–5 inches (10–12.5 cm). Be guided by the shape of the leaves. Near the stalk end, the pieces will form a cup shape.

5. Using either a round or oblong tablespoon as a mould, place a spoonful of the fish on to each piece of lettuce and arrange the filled leaves on a serving dish. Serve at room temperature. Let your guests pick up the leaves with their fingers, closing the sides as they do so to make the leaves into neat rolls.

Note: Steaming is an ancient Chinese cookery technique achieved by using either a wok set or a specially constructed metal steamer.

Using a wok set and metal trivet: Place the wok on its stand on top of the burner and set a metal trivet in the centre of the wok. Put the food to be steamed on a shallow heatproof dish with raised sides, so that the juices are retained in the dish when the food is cooked, thus preserving its goodness and taste. Place the dish on the metal trivet.

Now fill the wok with boiling water to within about 1 inch (2.5 cm) of the base of the dish so that the bubbling water does not get into the dish and spoil the food. Cover the wok with its lid, turn up the heat and maintain it at the same intensity to ensure that plenty of steam rises from the boiling water and circulates inside the covered wok to cook the food. If the food is to be steamed for a long time, for instance an hour, be sure to replenish the water from time to time. Refrain from lifting the wok lid unnecessarily, however, for every time you do so steam escapes and you will need to steam the food for a longer period to make sure it is cooked.

Using a wok set and bamboo steaming container: Place the wok on its stand on top of the burner and put in a slotted bamboo steaming container, large enough to wedge against the sloping sides of the wok. Fill the wok with boiling water to within 1 inch (2.5 cm) of the base of the container. Put the food to be steamed on a shallow heatproof dish with raised sides and place the dish in the bamboo container. Add the fitted bamboo lid and cover the wok with its lid, turn up the heat, and maintain it at the same intensity to ensure that plenty of steam rises from the boiling water and circulates inside the covered wok to cook the food. Again, if the food needs to be steamed for a long time, be sure to replenish the water from time to time.

Using a metal steamer: This is usually made of aluminium or stainless steel, round or oval in shape, and consists of a base container and two perforated steaming containers. Place the base container on top of the burner and half fill with boiling water. Put the food to be steamed on a heatproof dish with raised sides and place the dish into the steaming container. Put on the lid, turn up the heat and continue as for the wok set and metal trivet above.

CEVICHE

INGREDIENTS
2 lb (900 g) trout
8 oz (225 g) halibut fillet
2 lemons
2 limes
5 tablespoons dry vermouth
1 tablespoon chopped fresh dill
salt
1 lemon, cut into wedges
sprigs of fresh dill, for garnish

This is a foolproof adaptation of a classic dish. Your guests will find it particularly refreshing served ice-cold.

SERVES 15

1. Skin and bone the trout, making sure to remove all the tiny bones. Rinse both the trout and the halibut under cold running water and thoroughly pat dry with kitchen paper. Cut the fish into small bite-sized cubes and put them in a non-metallic bowl.

2. Using a zester, remove the rind from lemon and lime and chop it into fine dice. Squeeze the juice from both lemons and both limes and strain it into a jug. Add the diced lemon and lime rind, vermouth and chopped dill.

3. Pour the marinade over the fish, sprinkle with salt and chill for 6 hours, covered, stirring at intervals to ensure that the fish marinates evenly. When the fish is ready it will have taken on an opaque appearance.

4. Lift the fish out of the marinade using a slotted spoon and transfer it to a deep-sided serving dish. Garnish with some wedges of lemon and fresh dill sprigs. Provide cocktail sticks for your guests to spear the bite-sized cubes of fish.

Note: As it is to be served raw, make sure you use only the very freshest fish.

PRAWN, GINGER *and* SPINACH OMELETTES

INGREDIENTS

8 oz (225 g) frozen spinach,
    thawed and squeezed dry
knobs of butter
1 tablespoon ginger juice (see page
    13)
8 oz (225 g) peeled prawns
salt
freshly ground black pepper
4 large eggs
1 teaspoon salt
vegetable oil

This is one idea that was originally exported to the East from the West and we, in turn, adapted it back into our menus after working on the launch of a Japanese cookery book. These colourful omelettes make a versatile accompaniment to drinks. Try filling them with a purée of sautéed courgettes and toasted sesame seeds as an alternative to prawns, spinach and ginger.

SERVES 15

1. Toss the spinach and butter in a saucepan over a high heat for about 3 minutes. Let the spinach cool a little, then put it into the bowl of a food processor, add the ginger juice and process to a fine purée. Transfer the spinach purée to a mixing bowl.

2. Put the prawns in the processor and chop finely. Using a spatula, transfer the prawns to the bowl containing the spinach purée. Mix well and season with salt and black pepper, then set aside while you make the omelettes.

3. Break the eggs into a mixing bowl, add the salt and whisk until frothy. Set a 7 inch (17.5 cm) omelette pan over a high heat and add about a teaspoon of vegetable oil. Swirl the pan around to spread the oil evenly and pour any surplus into a ramekin or heatproof container. Ladle about 3 tablespoons of the egg mixture into the omelette pan, swirling the pan around to ensure that the mixture covers the surface evenly. Cook for 1 minute – or less – until the underside of the omelette is light brown in colour, easing around the edges of the omelette with a palette knife to prevent it from sticking. Carefully turn the omelette over and cook for a further 30 seconds, then remove the omelette from the pan and set aside to cool. Repeat the process until all of the egg mixture is used. You should be able to make six or seven omelettes.

4. Take one omelette and place it on a bamboo rolling mat – the end nearest you should be about 1 inch (2.5 cm) from the edge of the mat. Thinly spread the spinach and prawn mixture over the omelette. Lift the edge of the bamboo mat nearest you, turn the end over the edge of the omelette and start to roll up

the omelette tightly, making sure that the mat is not incorporated into the omelette roll. When the roll is completed, pull the mat and omelette together tightly to increase its firmness. Repeat with the remaining omelettes and filling mixture.

5. Cut the omelette rolls into 1 inch (2.5 cm) slices. Serve at room temperature, arranged on a platter for guests to pick up with their fingers.

Note: These omelettes would be attractive served with alternate rows of Spinach and Smoked Salmon Roulades (see page 22) or Glutinous Rice Rolls (see page 34). They would look particularly attractive served on a bed of aramé seaweed. This is a Japanese seaweed, readily available in health food stores and delicatessens. It is sold dried, and is prepared by soaking overnight.

MINIATURE PANCAKES

We often make these tiny pancakes in the morning of the day of a party for which we are catering and fill them at the same time. They do not lose any appearance and are as delicious as if they had been filled minutes before. Simply cover well and place in the refrigerator after preparation.

SERVES 20

INGREDIENTS

2 oz (50 g) plain flour
$\frac{1}{4}$ teaspoon salt
2 eggs, lightly beaten
$\frac{1}{2}$ pint (300 ml) milk
2 oz (50 g) unsalted butter, melted
about 3 oz (75 g) butter for frying
freshly ground black pepper
1 tablespoon freshly squeezed
    lemon juice
6 tablespoons soured cream
8 oz (225 g) smoked salmon, cut
    into fine strips
1 lime, thinly sliced

1. Sift the flour and salt into a bowl. Beat the eggs with the milk and melted butter and gradually whisk into the flour until the batter is smooth. Allow the batter to stand for at least an hour.

2. Put a knob of butter in a heavy frying pan or skillet over a medium heat and allow the butter to melt. Ladle about 3 tablespoons of batter into the pan and immediately swirl the pan around so that the batter spreads evenly over the surface. Cook for $1\frac{1}{2}$ minutes then, using a spatula, flip the pancake over and cook for a further $1\frac{1}{2}$ minutes. Remove the cooked pancake from the pan and set aside on a lightly floured surface. Continue making pancakes in this way until all the batter is used.

3. Lay out the pancakes, one at a time, on the work surface and cut out rounds using a 3 inch (7.5 cm) diameter pastry cutter. Stir the lemon juice into the soured cream and lightly spread the mixture on one side of each miniature pancake. Season with black pepper, then add two or three strips of smoked salmon. Do not put so much smoked salmon in a pancake that it is difficult to fold. Fold over each pancake into a semicircle – the soured cream will help it to stick together.

4. Cut each slice of lime into six wedges, then trim away the rind and pith. Garnish each pancake with a tiny segment of lime – this will enhance the flavour. Serve cold on a platter, allowing about three pancakes per guest.

SHELL-SERVED MUSSELS

This colourful Spanish tapas is not difficult to prepare and makes few demands in the way of ingredients. All the more reason, then, to use the very best olive oil that money can buy.

SERVES 20

INGREDIENTS
60 mussels
¼ pint (150 ml) white wine
3½ fl oz (100 ml) extra virgin olive oil, preferably Spanish
3 tablespoons red wine vinegar
2 tablespoons very finely chopped shallots
1 small sweet green pepper, skinned (see page 52), seeded and very finely chopped
1 small sweet red pepper, skinned (see page 52), seeded and very finely chopped
2 tablespoons finely chopped parsley
salt
freshly ground black pepper

1. Clean the mussels well, taking care to remove their beards. Discard any that are not firmly closed.

2. Place a large heavy-bottomed saucepan over a medium heat and pour in the white wine. Add the mussels to the pan and cover with a lid, then increase the heat and bring to the boil. Start to remove the mussels as they open and set them aside to cool. They should all be done in about 5 minutes – discard any that have not opened in that time.

3. When they are cool, remove the mussels from their shells. Retain half of the shells – the most presentable ones – and scrub them thoroughly.

4. In a bowl, beat together the oil and vinegar. Add the shallots, chopped peppers, half of the parsley, the salt and some black pepper, and mix well together. Stir in the mussels. Cover and keep in the refrigerator for 8 hours, turning the mussels in the vinaigrette from time to time.

5. When ready to serve, spoon each mussel into a cleaned mussel shell, making sure that each one has a flash of colour from the chopped peppers. Sprinkle each mussel with a little of the remaining parsley and serve on a large platter.

Note: The mussels can be left in the vinaigrette for up to 24 hours if you want to prepare them a day in advance.

FRAGRANT BRISKET

INGREDIENTS

3 lb (1.4 kg) piece salted brisket, about 3 inches (7.5 cm) wide
4 whole or 32 segments star anise
1 tablespoon Sichuan peppercorns
1½–2 teaspoons black peppercorns
2 inch (5 cm) cinnamon stick, broken up
1 large piece (¼ of whole) preserved tangerine peel
1 teaspoon cloves
1 small lump candy crystal sugar, or 1 teaspoon sugar
1 pint (600 ml) water

Brisket, a tasty and inexpensive cut of beef lending itself to long and slow cooking, is sold more often than not preserved in brine. Simmered in this combination of spices popular with the Chinese, the end result is an uncomplicated and homely food that goes well with drinks. That it is so easy to make and so labour-saving mustn't be overlooked. The brisket will shrink quite a lot with the cooking; this is why I've suggested using a broad strip.

SERVES 12

1. Submerge the bricket in cold water for 1–2 hours to rid it of some of the brine. Discard the soaking water.

2. Put the star anise, Sichuan peppercorns, black peppercorns, cinnamon stick, tangerine peel, cloves and sugar in a fire-proof casserole. Add the water and slowly bring to a simmer. Continue to simmer for about 20 minutes, allowing the aromas of the spices to be released.

3. Add the beef to the casserole. The spiced liquid should not come more than half way up the thickness of the beef. Return to a slow boil then reduce the heat to as low as possible and continue to simmer, with the lid on tightly, for 3–3½ hours. Turn over the brisket at the end of every hour so that the whole piece gets the simmering and steaming effect evenly. It should not be necessary to add more water. At the end of the cooking time, the meat should be very tender. Remove the meat from the casserole and discard any pieces of spice that are stuck to it. Allow to cool for about an hour.

4. To serve the meat, trim off the fat, cut into thin slices across the grain, and arrange on a serving dish. Serve at room temperature with cocktail sticks or bamboo forks, or let your guests use their fingers. Offer made-up hot mustard as a dipping sauce, if preferred.

Note: The brisket is also flavourful served cold, so it can be cooked in advance and kept, covered, in the refrigerator until required.

RIGHT: *Smoked Salmon Parcels*
(pages 18–19)

SMOKED LAMB

INGREDIENTS
3 tablespoons Dijon mustard
2 tablespoons thick Greek
  yoghurt
1 lb (900 g) smoked lamb

If you only have 15 minutes before your guests arrive and want to offer them a little more hospitality than a glass or two of wine, then provided you have been able to call in at a delicatessen on your way home, this is a novel and inexpensive idea with an unusual flavour.

SERVES 12–15

1. Combine the mustard and yoghurt in a small bowl. Cut each slice of smoked lamb in two, discarding any thin fatty pieces.

2. Thinly spread the lamb with the mustard and yoghurt mixture, concentrating most on the central part of the slices.

3. Roll up each slice into a small roulade, skewer with a cocktail stick and serve cold, with white wine.

LEFT: *Phyllo Pastry Tulips (pages 20–21)*

GLUTINOUS RICE ROLLS

This is a successful Sino-Japanese alliance on the culinary front. Glutinous rice, stir-fried the Chinese way, is usually served hot, but once wrapped in Japanese nori sheets, it can become a party food – none the less delicious served cold, and very pretty to look at as devised here. A flexible bamboo mat is essential equipment for this recipe, as it facilitates shaping the rolls. These mats are inexpensive and can be bought in kitchen and Oriental shops.

SERVES 20–25

INGREDIENTS

2 oz (50 g) dried shrimps, rinsed and soaked in 2 tablespoons warm water for 30 minutes

10 medium dried Chinese mushrooms, reconstituted (see page 13)

10 oz (275 g) lean pork, finely minced

1 lb (450 g) white glutinous rice

¼ teaspoon salt

6 tablespoons groundnut or vegetable oil

1¼ pints (750 ml) water

10 large spring onions, trimmed and cut into tiny rounds

½ tablespoon Shaoxing wine or medium dry sherry

4 oz (100 g) sliced ham, chopped into small dices

7–8 nori sheets, each about 8 × 7 inches (20 × 17.5 cm)

1 large bunch coriander, stalks removed, rinsed and pat dried

FOR THE MARINADE

¼ teaspoon salt

¼ teaspoon sugar

1 tablespoon thin or light soy sauce

freshly ground black or white pepper

1½ teaspoons Shaoxing wine or medium-dry sherry

1 teaspoon potato flour or arrowroot

1 tablespoon reserved shrimp-soaking liquid

1 tablespoon sesame oil

1. Drain the dried shrimps, reserving the soaking liquid, and chop them very finely. Drain the mushrooms and cut them into very small dice.

2. Put the pork in a large bowl. Add the salt, sugar, soy sauce, pepper, wine or sherry and potato flour or arrowroot for the marinade and mix well. Add the shrimp-soaking liquid and stir vigorously until absorbed. Leave to stand for 15–20 minutes, then stir in the sesame oil.

3. Rinse the rice about four times until the water is relatively clear, then put it in a heavy-bottomed saucepan with the salt, 2 tablespoons of the oil and the water. Put the lid on the pan and bring to the boil. Stir the rice a few times while the excess water is being absorbed, leaving only 'eyelets' around the rice, then put the saucepan on a metal heat deflector, reduce the heat to low and leave, covered, for about 15 minutes or until the rice is cooked through.

4. Meanwhile, stir-fry the pork. Heat a wok over a high heat until smoke rises, then add the remaining 4 tablespoons of oil and swirl it around. Add the spring onions and stir to release the aroma, add the dried shrimps and stir a few more times, then add the Chinese mushrooms and stir again. Next add the pork and, going to the bottom of the wok with a wok scoop or metal spatula, flip and turn for about 1 minute or until the pork is partially cooked and turning opaque. Splash in the wine or sherry around the side of the wok, continuing to stir for another minute or longer, until the pork is cooked through. Add the ham and stir to mix well, then scoop the mixture into a large dish or bowl.

5. Fluff up the rice and spoon it into the pork mixture. Mix thoroughly. Leave to stand for about 5 minutes.

6. While the mixture is still warm, make the rolls. Take a sheet of nori, hold it with your fingers and pass one side only over a low flame three or four times, until it becomes crisp. Toasting it this way enhances the flavour and improves the texture; otherwise the nori tends to be fishy and tough. Place the toasted nori sheet on a bamboo mat, shiny side down, the longer side across the mat and leaving a gap of about 1 inch (2.5 cm) on the mat near yourself. Evenly spread about 12 tablespoons of the rice mixture on the nori, reaching almost to the bottom edge and right and left-hand sides. Leave a gap of about $1\frac{1}{2}$ inches (4 cm) at the far side of the nori sheet. Spread a line of overlapping coriander leaves across the rice about $1\frac{1}{2}$ inches (4 cm) from the bottom of the nori.

7. Pick up the near edge of the mat, press it against the nori and start rolling. Continue to roll the nori with one hand and pick up the mat with the other (to ensure that the mat is not incorporated as part of the roll) until you are within 1 inch (2.5 cm) of the far side of the mat. Turn the mat (with the roll encased) over and give it a firm tug while you pull the rest of the mat away from yourself with your other hand.

8. Take the roll out of the mat and place it on a dish, removing any rice on the surface of the nori. Continue making rolls in this way until the rice mixture is used up. You may have to wash and dry the bamboo mat after making two or three rolls as the rice tends to stick to the matting. Chill the rolls in the refrigerator for about 2 hours. There is no need to cover the rolls since the nori acts as a protective skin.

9. To serve the rolls, trim off the untidy ends, then cut crossways into $\frac{1}{4}$ inch (5 mm) pieces, or however thick you may wish. Arrange on a serving dish and serve cold. Fingers are the best implements to pick them up with.

Note: The rolls can be made a day in advance. In that case they should be covered well before they are placed in the refrigerator, lest the rice becomes too dry. For illustrated instructions on making the rolls, see page 36.

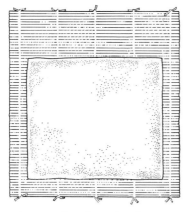

Place the toasted nori on a bamboo mat and leave a gap of about 2.5 cm on the side of the mat nearest to you.

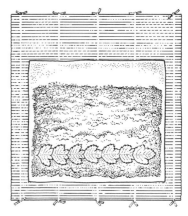

Spread the rice mixture evenly on the nori, reaching almost to the bottom edge and right and left-hand sides. Leave a gap of 4 cm at the far side of the nori sheet, and spread a line of overlapping coriander leaves about 4 cm from the bottom of the nori.

Pick up the near edge of the mat, press it against the nori, and push gently so that the nori rolls up underneath.

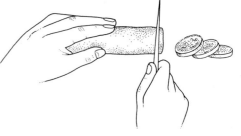

When the rolls have been chilled, trim off the untidy ends, then cut crossways in 5 mm pieces.

STUFFED CHICKEN BREASTS

INGREDIENTS

4 chicken breasts, skinned and
   boned
8 radicchio leaves, washed and
   dried
8 thin slices of coppa or Parma
   ham
¼ pint (150 ml) white wine
¼ pint (150 ml) chicken stock
freshly ground black pepper
lamb's lettuce or watercress, for
   garnish

*If your cocktail party promises to be longer than the traditional
2 hours, you may need to provide something a little more substantial as part of the menu. These inviting chicken rounds are
just the thing. For best results, make them a day in advance and
allow two or three rounds per guest.*

SERVES 15

1. Place a chicken breast between two sheets of foil and beat it
out into a thin escalope using a rolling pin. Peel off the foil and
spread two radicchio leaves over the escalope – this will ensure
that the chicken stays moist. On to this, press two slices of coppa
(this is used in preference to other Italian meats as it has more
veins of fat and will be more flavoursome). Lightly roll up the
chicken breast to form a thin roll and secure with cocktail sticks.
Make three more rolls in the same way, then wrap the rolls in
foil and refrigerate for 30 minutes.

2. Put the wine and stock into a wide, shallow saucepan and
warm through over a medium heat. Place the chicken breast rolls
in the saucepan, cover and poach for 5 minutes. Set aside to cool
in the liquid for about 30 minutes.

3. Drain the chicken breasts. Remove the foil and cut the rolls
into ½ inch (1.25 cm) slices. Arrange the rounds on a platter, either
with a selection of other savouries or on their own. Sprinkle
with a little black pepper and garnish with lamb's lettuce or
watercress.

Note: The flavour improves if the cooked chicken is left to stand
for an hour or so, at room temperature, before it is unwrapped
and sliced.

GLAZED CHICKEN

Very exotic sweet and sour chicken cubes glazed in a sauce of mango chutney, lime, ginger and garlic, and achieved by the stir-frying technique. A nibble that will make you ask for white wine, which in turn will whet your appetite – making the chicken all the more irresistible.

SERVES 12–15

INGREDIENTS

1½ lb (675 g) skinned and boned chicken breasts

6 fl oz (175 ml) groundnut or vegetable oil

4–5 teaspoons very finely chopped garlic

4 teaspoons finely shredded fresh ginger root

1 tablespoon Shaoxing wine or medium dry sherry

small bunch coriander leaves for garnish

FOR THE MARINADE

1 teaspoon salt

½ teaspoon sugar

1½–2 tablespoons thin or light soy sauce

freshly ground black or white pepper to taste

2 teaspoons Shaoxing wine or medium dry sherry

2 teaspoons cornflour

1½ tablespoons egg white, lightly beaten

1 tablespoon groundnut or vegetable oil

1 tablespoon sesame oil

FOR THE SAUCE

6 tablespoons mango chutney

3 tablespoons freshly squeezed lime juice

2 teapoons thin or light soy sauce

1. Cut the chicken into ¾ inch (2 cm) cubes and put them into a bowl. Add the salt, sugar, soy sauce, pepper and wine or sherry for the marinade and mix well. Sprinkle on the cornflour, add the egg white and stir until they have been absorbed. Leave to marinate for 20–30 minutes. Stir in the oils.

2. To make the sauce, chop up the lumps of mango in the chutney, then stir in the lime juice and soy sauce. Set aside.

3. When the chicken is ready, heat a wok over a high heat until plenty of smoke rises. Add the oil and swirl it around for several seconds, then add the chicken and stir, separating the pieces, for about 1 minute. The chicken will turn whitish, being partially cooked. Remove the wok from the heat and, using a perforated spoon, scoop the chicken on to a dish and set aside, leaving the oil behind in the wok.

4. Reheat the oil in the wok over a high heat until smoke rises. Add the garlic, stir, then add the ginger and stir again. Pour in the sauce and stir to mix until hot.

5. Return the chicken to the wok, and turn and toss in the sauce for about 30 seconds, or until very hot again. Splash in the wine around the side of the wok. The sizzling enhances the fragrance and quickens the cooking. Stir a few more times – the chicken should be completely cooked by now.

6. Scoop the chicken on to a serving dish, and garnish with the bunch of coriander leaves. Serve immediately. Toothpicks or small bamboo forks can be used to pick up the cubes of chicken.

CHICKEN LIVER PÂTÉ on CUCUMBER

INGREDIENTS
1 lb (450 g) chicken livers
3½ fl oz (100 ml) olive oil
2 large cloves garlic, roughly
   chopped
2 tablespoons Cognac
½–¾ teaspoon salt
1 tablespoon thin or light soy
   sauce
1 teaspoon dried thyme
1 teaspoon dried marjoram
freshly ground black pepper
2 large cucumbers

An inexpensive eat that goes well with a glass of sherry or white wine. One can, of course, spread the pâté on rounds or squares of toast, but I find that can be rather dry on the palate. Spreading it on cucumber slices, on the other hand, gives a pleasing combination.

SERVES 20–30

1. Cut each chicken liver into two or three pieces, following its lobes. Remove the white membranes and clotted blood.

2. Heat a wok or sauté pan until hot, then pour in the olive oil and heat until hot. Add the garlic, stir two or three times, then add the chicken livers. Stir for about 30 seconds, until the livers become partially opaque. Add the Cognac and let it sizzle for a few seconds. Season with the salt, soy sauce, thyme and marjoram, and stir to mix. Reduce the heat to medium and continue to cook, covered, for 3½–4 minutes, or until the livers are just done and still slightly pink in the centre. Remove the pan from the heat.

3. Scoop the contents of the pan into a food processor and process to a smooth purée, adding some black pepper. Transfer the pâté to a serving bowl or pâté dish, and leave to cool thoroughly.

4. Cut the cucumbers into rounds about ⅛ inch (3 mm) thick. On each round, spread a layer of pâté about as thick as the cucumber itself, preferably leaving a clean border for better appearance. Arrange the rounds on a serving dish and serve cold.

Note: The finished canapés will keep well cling-filmed in the refrigerator for up to 2 hours. Alternatively, just make the pâté in advance. If it is not to be used on the same day, pour 2–3 oz (50–75 g) of clarified butter over the surface to keep it moist. The pâté can then be stored in the refrigerator for about a week.

AROMATIC TEA EGGS (1) CHICKEN'S EGGS

INGREDIENTS

18 small eggs
2 tablespoons jasmine tea leaves
1 pint (600 ml) water
1½–1¾ teaspoons salt
2 tablespoons thin or light soy
   sauce
2 teaspoons sugar
1½ whole or 12 segments star anise
1½ inch (4 cm) cinnamon stick
slivers of red pepper or finely
   chopped parsley to garnish

Aromatic tea eggs, with their marbled porcelain appearance, are very popular with the Chinese. Traditionally, chicken's eggs are used, and they are usually served whole. For cocktail parties in the West I have suggested halving the eggs and piping on the egg yolk filling.

These are the traditional tea eggs, beloved of Shanghai people. Usually served whole, their greatest appeal to the Chinese eye lies in the crackles on the egg white, reminiscent of Chinese porcelain. Served this way, however, the hard-boiled yolks tend to be dry and lacking in taste. By mashing the yolk with a little of the aromatic liquid and then piping it back on to the egg white, I have made the eggs more moist, thus more appealing both to the eye and to the palate.

SERVES 12–15

1. Wash the eggs if there are any impurities on the shells. Pierce each egg with a pin once to prevent cracking, then put the eggs into a large saucepan, cover with plenty of cold water and gently bring to the boil. Continue to cook for about 5 minutes. Remove the eggs from the pan and submerge in cold water for a few minutes.

2. Boil the tea leaves in the water for about 5 minutes in order to extract the essence from them. Strain the tea and discard the leaves.

3. Gently crack the egg shells by applying pressure from the palm and rolling the eggs, one by one, on a table; alternatively, use a spoon and tap over the shell. Put the eggs into a saucepan, preferably large enough to hold them in a single layer. Pour in the tea, and add the salt, soy sauce, sugar, star anise and cinnamon. If the liquid is not sufficient to cover the eggs, add some water. Bring to the boil, then reduce the heat to medium and cook gently, covered, for about 30 minutes, reducing the liquid to about 1 pint (600 ml) again. Remove the saucepan from the heat and allow the liquid to cool to room temperature. Remove the eggs, strain the liquid and discard the solids.

4. Shell the eggs and halve them lengthways. Carefully remove the yolks and put them in a bowl with a small amount of the cooling liquid – about 1 teaspoon per whole yolk. Mash to a smooth consistency. Spoon the mashed yolk into a piping bag and, holding the bag firmly in one hand, force the mixture down into the nozzle. In short bursts, squeeze the mixture into the centre of the egg whites.

5. Arrange the egg halves on a platter and garnish with slivers of red pepper or finely chopped parsley. Serve either at room temperature or cold. Fingers are the best implements to pick them up with.

Note: These eggs can be made several hours in advance and refrigerated covered with clingfilm.

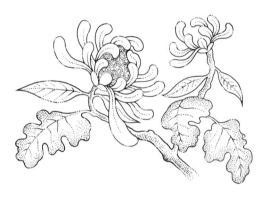

(II) QUAILS' EGGS

INGREDIENTS

48 quails' eggs
2 tablespoons jasmine tea leaves
1 pint (600 ml) water
1½ teaspoons salt
2 tablespoons thin or light soy
    sauce
2 teaspoons sugar
1½ whole or 12 segments star anise
1½ inch (4 cm) cinnamon stick

Quails' eggs are small and in China they are not used for making the traditional aromatic tea eggs. They appear either as a garnish or as a contrast to another ingredient with a crunchy texture.

These quails' eggs are steeped in aromatic tea, which gives them an enticing flavour and a delicately marbled appearance. Don't be disheartened if the marbling is faint – the flavour will be none the less impressive.

SERVES 12–15

1. Put the eggs into a large saucepan, cover with plenty of cold water, gently bring to the boil and continue to cook over a low heat for 45–60 seconds. Remove from the heat, pour the eggs into a large colander and refresh them under cold running water. This separates the skin from the egg white, ensuring easier peeling later.

2. Boil the tea leaves in the water for about 5 minutes in order to extract the essence from them. Strain the tea and discard the leaves.

3. Gently crack the egg shells by applying pressure from the palm and rolling the eggs, one by one, on a table. This results in a network of fine cracks on the shell.

4. Put all the eggs into a saucepan large enough to hold them in a single layer. Pour in the tea, and add the salt, soy sauce, sugar, star anise and cinnamon stick. If the liquid is not sufficient to cover the eggs, add some water. Gently bring to the boil, reduce the heat and simmer, covered, for 20–25 minutes. Remove from the heat and leave the eggs in the liquid for about 6 hours or overnight, allowing the liquid which has seeped through the cracks inside the eggs to continue to season them.

5. Shortly before serving, remove the eggs from the liquid and carefully peel off their shells. Serve cold or at room temperature, for your guests to pick up with their fingers. The liquid itself is not served.

Note: The unshelled eggs will keep well in the refrigerator for 3–4 days.

STUFFED LYCHEES

INGREDIENTS
25 canned lychees, drained
about 4 oz (100 g) Roquefort
cheese
slivers of sweet red pepper, for
garnish

East may be East and West may be West, but if Rudyard Kipling had tasted these sweet lychees stuffed with strong Roquefort cheese, even he might have agreed that sometimes the twain shall meet. Canned lychees, rather than fresh ones, are used because of their reliable syrupy sweetness, a complementary contrast to the Roquefort, which is extremely strong in taste.

I have tried out several different cheeses, including Stilton – one of my very favourite cheeses – and other blue cheeses such as Danish Blue and Gorgonzola, but none of them works as well. Only the Roquefort with the lychee can accomplish the ideal yin and yang savoury sweetness.

SERVES 6–8

1. Stand the drained lychees on kitchen paper, turning them over and replacing the paper several times to get rid of all excess moisture.

2. Meanwhile mash the cheese with a fork or spoon, mixing the green with the white.

3. Using a small palate knife, fill the hollow of each lychee with as much cheese as possible. The cheese can actually be used to cement a torn lychee, making it whole again. Place a sliver of red pepper on top of each to enhance the visual appeal.

4. Cover the lychees with cling film and chill in the refrigerator until ready to serve. Serve very cold.

Note: They may be kept in the refrigerator for up to 24 hours.

SPINACH BARQUETTES

INGREDIENTS
1 lb (450 g) fresh spinach,
   thoroughly washed, stems
   discarded
1½ oz (40 g) butter
salt
freshly ground black pepper
grated nutmeg
3 fl oz (90 ml) double cream,
   whipped
paprika, to decorate

FOR THE PASTRY
6 oz (175 g) plain flour
pinch of salt
3 oz (75 g) butter, chilled and
   cubed
2 tablespoons cold water

These tiny barquettes are a light and delicious combination. There really is no substitute for the unmistakable flavour and texture of fresh spinach in this recipe, even though it does mean slightly more work than the frozen variety. There are a number of ways to prepare fresh spinach. I find that the best way is to wash the spinach thoroughly under running cold water, then throw the leaves into a heavy-bottomed saucepan, or wok, adding a generous knob of butter. Place the lid on the saucepan, and move the pan firmly over the heat for about 5 minutes. No water is needed, as the water in the spinach evaporates during the cooking. If you like the particularly strong flavour of iron, then leave a generous amount of stalk on each leaf.

SERVES 10

1. First make the pastry. Sift the flour and salt into a bowl, add the butter and rub in with your fingertips until the mixture resembles fine crumbs. Blend in the water, using a fork. Gather the dough together into a ball and wrap it in foil or cling film, then refrigerate for at least 30 minutes.

2. Heat the oven to 375°F/190°C/gas mark 5 and lightly oil about 20 barquette moulds. Roll out the pastry thinly and line the moulds, pricking the base and sides of the pastry with a fork. Place the barquette moulds on a baking sheet and bake in the oven for about 15 minutes, until the pastry is firm and lightly coloured. When they have cooled slightly, slide the pastry cases out of the moulds and set aside on a wire rack.

3. To make the spinach filling, shake the surplus water from the washed leaves and put them in a large saucepan. Bring to the boil and simmer gently, uncovered, for about 10 minutes, or until tender. Drain the spinach and purée it in a food processor.

4. Melt the butter in a saucepan over a medium heat and sauté the spinach purée for 6–7 minutes, to drive off excess moisture. Season with salt, pepper and nutmeg, then set aside to cool.

5. Fold the cream into the spinach purée and fill the barquettes. Serve at once, decorated with a little paprika.

Note: The pastry cases can be cooked in advance and will freeze well, stored in a plastic container. To defrost, allow an hour at room temperature. The spinach purée can be made a day ahead and kept in the refrigerator in a covered bowl, but don't add the cream until you are ready to fill the barquettes.

Spinach Barquettes.

CHOUX PUFFS *with* SPICED AVOCADO

INGREDIENTS
3 avocados
1 tablespoon freshly squeezed
   lemon juice
freshly ground black pepper
2 tablespoons crème fraîche
4 tomatoes, skinned, seeded and
   chopped
2 spring onions, finely chopped
1 tablespoon sweet chilli sauce

FOR THE CHOUX PASTRY
$\frac{1}{4}$ pint (150 ml) water
$1\frac{1}{2}$ oz (40 g) butter
$\frac{1}{4}$–$\frac{1}{2}$ level teaspoon salt
$2\frac{1}{2}$ oz (65 g) plain flour
2 large eggs
1 small egg, beaten with 1
   tablespoon of milk, to glaze

This is good party food to prepare for large numbers because, of all pastries, choux is the easiest to produce in quantity. Though typecast by its normally sweet role, the otherwise bland choux is a perfect foil for the hot aftertaste of this spicy avocado filling. It is certainly worthwhile mastering the relatively simple art of making choux pastry, as, unlike other types of pastry, there are, as yet, no ready-made brands available.

SERVES 15

1. First make the choux puffs. Put the water into a heavy-bottomed saucepan, add the butter and bring to the boil. When the butter has melted, add the salt. Remove the pan from the heat and quickly add the flour. Stir to a smooth consistency, then return the pan to a high heat and continue to stir until the thickened mixture is a smooth, soft dough that can be rolled around the pan. Transfer the dough to a mixing bowl and set aside for 5 minutes.

2. Add the 2 large eggs to the dough in the mixing bowl one at a time, beating them in thoroughly. When both eggs have been added and the dough is smooth and shiny, cover the bowl with cling film and leave to stand at room temperature for 1–2 hours.

3. Heat the oven to 425°F/220°C/gas mark 7 and lightly grease two baking sheets. Spoon the dough into a piping bag fitted with a $\frac{1}{2}$ inch (12.5 cm) nozzle, and pipe mounds of about 1 inch (2.5 cm) diameter and $\frac{1}{2}$ inch (1.25 cm) height on to the baking sheets. Brush with the egg and milk glaze.

4. Bake the choux puffs in the oven for 8–10 minutes, until light golden in colour. Reduce the oven temperature to 325°F/170°C/gas mark 3 and bake for another 15 minutes, or until the puffs are golden brown, then turn off the oven and leave the puffs inside for a further 3 minutes. Remove the puffs from the oven and pierce each one with a skewer before placing on a wire rack to cool.

5. Peel and stone the avocados and put them into the bowl of a

food processor. Add the lemon juice, black pepper and crème fraîche and process to a smooth purée. Turn the mixture into a bowl and add the tomatoes, spring onions and chilli sauce. Combine all the ingredients together thoroughly.

6. Partly cut open each choux puff – make an incision large enough for you to spoon in the avocado mixture. Fill each puff with a generous teaspoonful so that the filling peeps out from the choux. Arrange the filled puffs on a platter and decorate with tiny sprigs of parsley if you feel this extra decoration is needed. Alternatively, arrange the puffs in rows on a large platter with a selection of other cold savouries.

Note: The choux puffs may be cooked in advance and stored in an airtight container for 2–3 days.

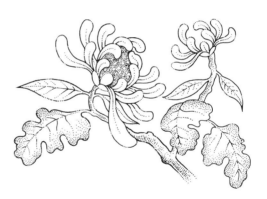

ASPARAGUS *with a* CLAM *and* LIME SAUCE

Boiled asparagus is simply too good merely to accompany a main course and we prefer to serve it as an hors d'oeuvre. This combination of flavours blends surprisingly well. Clam juice can be found in most shops that sell West Indian foods.

SERVES 15

INGREDIENTS

30 asparagus spears, about 5
    inches (12.5 cm) long
3 tablespoons clam juice
2 tablespoons dry white wine
juice of 2 limes
2 egg yolks
1 tablespoon double cream
salt
freshly ground black pepper
cayenne pepper
¾ oz (20 g) cold unsalted butter,
    diced

1. Trim the asparagus spears into even 4 inch (10 cm) lengths and cook in boiling salted water for about 12 minutes, or until tender. Drain the asparagus, reserving 4 tablespoons of the cooking liquid, and refresh immediately under cold running water. Set aside while you make the sauce.

2. Put the clam juice, white wine and lime juice into a small saucepan and cook until reduced by two-thirds. Add the egg yolks, reserved asparagus cooking liquid and cream. Whisk the sauce over a very low heat until it is light, thick and creamy.

3. Season the sauce with salt, black pepper and cayenne, then gradually whisk in the butter. This will thicken the sauce and heighten the flavour.

4. Cut each asparagus spear diagonally into two shorter pieces and arrange them on a platter. Turn the warm clam sauce into a bowl and serve with the asparagus as a dip.

RIGHT: *Spinach and Smoked Salmon Roulades (pages 22–23), Courgette and Chaumes on Pumpernickel (page 88), Char Siu Tartlets (pages 76–77)*

Spicy Cucumber

INGREDIENTS

2 large cucumbers, about 1 lb
 (450 g) each
4 teaspoons salt
4 tablespoons Chinese rice
 vinegar or 3 tablespoons white
 wine vinegar
6 tablespoons sugar
2 tablespoons sesame oil
1 tablespoon groundnut or
 vegetable oil
3–6 dried red chillies, seeded and
 cut into pieces

This is one of the most popular dishes I have ever devised, with universal appeal to one and all. Harmoniously salty, sweet, vinegary and as spicy-hot as you would wish, these crisp little snacks also keep well in the refrigerator 'for ever' – certainly several weeks!

SERVES 10–20

1. Quarter the cucumbers lengthways. Scoop out and discard the seeds, then cut the cucumber quarters crossways into $\frac{3}{4}$ inch (2 cm) pieces. Put them into a clean, grease-free bowl, sprinkle with the salt and stir to mix, then leave to stand at room temperature for 2–3 hours. During this time moisture from the cucumber will be drawn out.

2. Drain the cucumber, then squeeze out excess moisture either by hand or in a salad spinner but do not overdry. Transform to a clean bowl, add the vinegar and sugar, and mix well.

3. Heat the oils in a small saucepan until smoke rises. Remove the pan from the heat and wait for a few seconds until the smoke has disappeared before adding the chillies – otherwise they will be burned. Let the chillies sizzle in the oil, then pour them into the bowl with the cucumber and mix well.

4. Leave the cucumber to stand for at least 6 hours or overnight. Serve cold, with cocktail sticks.

Note: The cucumber will keep well, in the refrigerator, covered, for several weeks.

LEFT: *Palate-Cleansing Mange-Tout (page 56), Quails' Eggs – Aromatic Tea Eggs (page 42)*

CANAPÉ TOASTS

INGREDIENTS
12 thin slices white bread

FOR THE CURRIED LEEK TOPPING
2 oz (50 g) butter
4 leeks, washed thoroughly
1 teaspoon curry powder
2 eating apples, peeled, cored and
    sliced
2 oz (50 g) mozzarella, thinly
    sliced

FOR THE OLIVE PASTE TOPPING
30 pitted green olives
2 anchovies
2 teaspoons finely ground
    almonds
2 cloves garlic, crushed to a paste
1 teaspoon capers
3 tablespoons extra virgin olive
    oil, preferably Spanish
small pinch ground cummin
large pinch paprika
½ teaspoon chopped fresh thyme
freshly ground black pepper
slivers of skinned sweet red
    pepper, for garnish

Easy items that can be prepared in advance are vital to a well-balanced party menu, preferably in large quantities. This allows you time to attend to any items that must be prepared at the last minute. These two ideas for canapé toasts are among our most popular with guests, although the possible variations are endless.

SERVES 15

1. To make the toasts, first heat the oven to 400°F/200°C/gas mark 6. Using a 1½ inch (4 cm) pastry cutter, cut out four rounds from each slice of bread and place the bread rounds on a wire rack, lining them up in rows about ½ inch (1.25 cm) apart. Bake in the upper part of the oven for about 10 minutes, until a light golden brown colour. Remove the rack of toasts from the oven and set aside to cool.

2. Put the apples in a saucepan with half of the butter and cook to a purée over medium heat – this will take about 4 minutes.

3. Melt the remaining butter in a heavy-bottomed saucepan over a medium heat, add the leeks and sauté for about 2 minutes, until cooked through but not coloured. Stir in the curry powder and the apple purée, and cook for a further 2 minutes. Remove the pan from the heat and set aside.

4. Place all of the ingredients for the olive paste topping, except the red pepper slivers, in the bowl of a food processor and blend to a paste. Make sure that the paste is completely smooth.

5. Turn the olive paste into a small bowl and spread a generous amount on half of the toasts. Garnish each olive paste toast with a strip of red pepper to complement its colour, and arrange the toasts on a large circular platter or tray, leaving room to add the curried leek toasts when they are ready to serve.

6. Cut the slices of mozzarella into ½ inch (1.25 cm) squares. Spread the remaining toasts generously with the leek and apple mixture and top each one with a square of mozzarella. Arrange the toasts carefully on a rack and place under a hot grill for 30–45 seconds only – just long enough for the cheese to soften. Alternatively, arrange the toasts on a suitable dish and micro-

wave at full power for 20 seconds. Serve the curried leek toasts hot, on the platter with the olive paste toasts.

Note: The toast rounds can be prepared up to 3 days in advance and stored in an airtight container until required. The leek and apple mixture can also be prepared 3 days in advance and stored in an airtight container in the refrigerator. The olive paste is best made immediately before serving, but may be stored for up to 24 hours in a covered container in the refrigerator.

SWEET PEPPER SALAD

INGREDIENTS
9 large sweet peppers, a mixture
  of green, red and yellow
1½ tablespoons cooked groundnut
  oil (see page 13)
1 tablespoon sesame oil
1½ tablespoons thin or light soy
  sauce

*The alliance of Middle Eastern technique – grilling the peppers
until charred – and Chinese seasoning in this recipe works
wonders for these peppers.*

SERVES 15

1. Put the peppers on a rack under the hottest grill until the skin
becomes charred. This can take as long as 20 minutes, during
which time you should rotate the peppers occasionally so that
the skin darkens evenly. You may need to grill the peppers in
two lots if the rack is not large enough.

2. Remove the peppers from the heat and plunge them into cold
water. Peel off the skin, which should come off very easily.
Discard the hard top and stalk and the seeds inside. Pat dry the
peppers if necessary. Slice the flesh into large pieces and place in
a dish or bowl.

3. Add the oils and the soy sauce, and mix well. The smoky
taste from grilling will be enhanced and a subtle savoury quality
will be added to the sweetness of the pepper. Serve either at
room temperature or chilled. The slices can be picked up using
cocktail sticks or bamboo forks. Provide your guests with
napkins, too, to catch any drips of oil.

Note: The peppers can, alternatively, be baked in a preheated
oven at maximum temperature for 30–40 minutes until the skin
blisters. Done this way, they will be more watery when peeled
and will need to be carefully pat dried before the oils and soy
sauce are added.

MARINATED VEGETABLES

INGREDIENTS
8 oz (225 g) celeriac, peeled
6 sticks celery, trimmed,
    1 mooli (white radish), peeled
1 small cauliflower
4 oz (100 g) broccoli
1 sweet red pepper, seeded
12 tiny button onions
4 oz (100 g) mange-tout
8 oz (225 g) Emmental, very thinly
    sliced

FOR THE MARINADE
about ½ pint (300 ml) water
¾ pint (450 ml) dry white wine
6 tablespoons olive oil
3 tablespoons white wine vinegar
juice and grated rind of 2 limes
juice and grated rind of 1 lemon
1 tablespoon ginger juice (see page
    13)
3 cloves garlic, finely chopped
1½ tablespoons muscovado sugar
4 sprigs fresh mint
1 bay leaf
1 bouquet garni
1 tablespoon salt
8 coriander seeds
1 tablespoon turmeric

Don't be put off by the long list of ingredients for this recipe – it really couldn't be simpler, the almost-pickled vegetables will keep for 2 or 4 days in the refrigerator. Naturally, you can alter the ingredients according to what you have available.

SERVES 20

1. Cut the celeriac, celery and radish into pieces about 3 inches (7.5 cm) long and ¼ inch (6 mm) thick, divide the cauliflower and broccoli into bite-sized florets, and slice the red pepper into ¼ inch (6 mm) strips.

2. Combine all the ingredients for the marinade in a large saucepan and bring to the boil. Simmer for 5 minutes over a medium–low heat, then add the celeriac and simmer for a further 3 minutes. Next add the celery, radish, cauliflower and onions, and simmer, covered, for 5 minutes. You may need to add extra water to cover the vegetables. Add the broccoli and sweet pepper to the pan and continue to simmer, covered, for another 3 minutes, then add the mange-tout and cook for a final minute.

3. Remove the saucepan from the heat and pour the contents into a large bowl. Leave the vegetables to cool in the marinade – this will take about 1½ hours. When the marinade has cooled, put the bowl in the refrigerator and chill for 12 hours.

4. About an hour before your guests arrive, drain the vegetables. The marinade makes a delicious dressing for salads, so don't discard it: keep it in a covered jar in the refrigerator. Lightly dab dry the vegetables with kitchen paper and arrange them at one side of a large platter (you will probably have enough for two platters). At the other side of the platter, arrange overlapping slices of Emmental. Your guests can then take a slice of cheese and wrap it around a piece of marinated vegetable. Provide your guests with napkins.

Note: These vegetables are also excellent served with Yan-kit's Aromatic Chicken Eggs (see page 40) instead of the cheese.

MUSTARD-PICKLED AUBERGINE

This spicy dish is an unusual way to serve aubergines. Other salient points are that it can be prepared up to 24 hours in advance, needs no cooking and must be served cold.

SERVES 10

INGREDIENTS

2 aubergines, weighing 8–10 oz
(225–275 g) each
2¼ pints (1.3 litres) water
1½ tablespoons salt

FOR THE DRESSING

1½ tablespoons dry mustard
6 tablespoons shoyu
6 tablespoons mirin
6 tablespoons brown sugar

1. Cut the ends off the aubergines and cut each aubergine in half lengthways. Slice each half into ⅛ inch (3 mm) semicircular slices, then cut each slice in half again. Put the aubergine wedges into a large bowl, add the water and salt, and leave to soak for an hour. This will ensure that any bitter taste is removed.

2. In the meantime, prepare the dressing. Combine all of the ingredients in a mixing bowl and whisk thoroughly.

3. Drain the aubergines in a colander and lay out the pieces on kitchen paper. Pat dry thoroughly as too much moisture will impair the flavour.

4. Whisk the dressing once more, then add the aubergines to the bowl. Cover with cling film and refrigerate for about 4 hours to allow the flavours to develop.

5. When ready to serve, remove the aubergines from the dressing with a slotted spoon and dab dry with kitchen paper. Arrange the pieces of aubergine attractively on a platter and pour over a little of the dressing. Serve accompanied by napkins and cocktail sticks.

SALSIFY

INGREDIENTS
2 pints (1.2 litres) water
3 fl oz (90 ml) white wine vinegar
2 lb (900 g) black-skinned salsify
1½ oz (40 g) plain flour
1 teaspoon salt
5 tablespoons vegetable oil

Now readily available in large supermarkets, this once-popular vegetable is returning to fashion. It has a subtle taste which goes particularly well with dry sherry and is ideal if you do not want to serve anything too filling.

SERVES 15

1. Put the water into a bowl and add the vinegar. Carefully remove the outer bark-like skin from the salsify using a potato peeler. (You will find the skin is slightly sticky.) Rinse the salsify under cold running water and immediately submerge it in the acidulated water to prevent discoloration. Once all the salsify has been peeled, leave it in the water for 20 minutes.

2. Pour about 3 pints (1.75 litres) of cold water into a large saucepan. In a bowl, beat together the flour, salt and oil to form a paste, then whisk the paste into the water in the saucepan. Drain the salsify, add it to the pan, bring to the boil and cook, covered for 30 minutes.

3. Drain the salsify in a colander and refresh under cold running water. Pat dry with kitchen paper. Cut each piece of salsify into 2 inch (5 cm) lengths and serve simply on a platter for your guests to pick up with their fingers.

PALATE-CLEANSING MANGE-TOUT

After serving several deep-fried or rich, creamy eats, these totally plain mange-tout may be served to palate-cleansing effect. By adding salt and oil to the water when blanching the mange-tout, you will find that they retain their vivid colour for several hours.

SERVES 15–20

INGREDIENTS
1 tablespoon salt
2 tablespoons vegetable oil
1 lb (450 g) mange-tout, topped
   and tailed

1. Half fill a wok or large saucepan with water and bring to the boil. Add the salt and the oil and return to a rolling boil. Submerge the mange-tout in the water and continue to cook over a high heat until just before the water returns to the boil.

2. Pour the mange-tout into a colander and immediately refresh under cold running water. This will make the mange-tout crisp and shiny. Drain thoroughly.

3. Arrange the mange-tout on a serving dish, and serve either cold or chilled.

SPICY PEANUTS

INGREDIENTS
6 oz (175 g) cornflour
¼ pint (150 ml) water
1 lb (450 g) red-skinned peanuts
4 oz (100 g) plain flour
oil for deep-frying
1–2 teaspoons spiced salt (see
    page 13)
1–2 teaspoons hot oil

Hot and spicy, made the more crunchy by the outer skin and flour coating, these peanuts which are often found as a titbit on the tables in Sichuan restaurants are a perfect accompaniment for pre-dinner drinks when you do not want to serve anything too substantial. For a drinks party, no matter how many other items of eats you may have, these peanuts are always a welcome addition. Make double the quantity in one go – they will stay crisp for at least 2 weeks if stored in an airtight container.

SERVES 10–20

1. Put the cornflour in a large bowl and slowly add the water to make a gluey batter, stirring all the time with a fork or wooden spoon to prevent lumps from forming. Add all the peanuts to the bowl and stir to coat evenly with the batter. Turn the peanuts into a sieve to allow excess batter to drip off.

2. Pour the plain flour into a large bowl and add the peanuts. Press the flour over them until they have a snow-capped appearance. Transfer the floured nuts to a large wide-meshed sieve set over a basin and lightly shake off any excess flour, taking care not to shake off the snowy coating.

3. Fill the wok just under half full with oil, otherwise the oil may spill over when the peanuts are added. Heat the oil to a temperature of 375°F (190°C), carefully tip in the peanuts – the oil will foam momentarily. Moving the peanuts around from time to time with long chopsticks or a wooden spoon, deep-fry for about 8 minutes or until the oil reaches 350°F (180°C) again. The peanuts, with their partial coating of flour, will become crunchy. Remove the nuts from the wok using a large hand strainer or perforated spoon, and spread them out on kitchen paper to drain off excess cooking oil. Transfer to a bowl and sprinkle with the spiced salt and hot oil. Serve the peanuts warm or cold.

Note: If you are intending to deep-fry another batch at this stage, allow the loose flour in the oil to settle for 15–20 minutes, then pour the oil into another container. Discard the sediment in the bottom of the wok, then return the oil to the wok and reheat to the required temperature.

HOT
PARTY EATS

HAKE PUFFS

The sight of trays of cold vol-au-vents with gluey fillings has become the open dread of any party guest. It is a great pity, since these tiny pastry puffs can be most appetising. The delicate hake puff is a cousin of the vol-au-vent and reminiscent of its original creamy splendour.

SERVES 10

INGREDIENTS
1 lb (450 g) skinned hake fillet
2 oz (50 g) carrots
2 oz (50 g) celery
2 oz (50 g) leek
2 oz (50 g) butter
6 tablespoons fish stock
6 tablespoons double cream
2 tablespoons vermouth
salt
freshly ground black pepper

FOR THE PASTRY
8 oz (225 g) plain flour
pinch of salt
6 oz (175 g) cold butter
1 teaspoon freshly squeezed
   lemon juice
about 3 tablespoons cold water
milk for brushing

1. First make the pastry as described on page 46, step 1. Wrap the pastry in cling film and place in the refrigerator while you prepare the filling for the puffs.

2. Cut the carrots, celery and leek into fine julienne strips about 1 inch (2.5 cm) in length, then blanch in boiling salted water for 1 minute. Drain and refresh immediately under cold running water. Leave the vegetables to drain.

3. Cut the hake into short thin strips. Melt the butter in a saucepan and sauté the carrots, celery and leeks for 2 minutes, until just cooked. Add the hake and cook for a further 2 minutes, then add the stock, cream and vermouth. Bring to the boil and cook for 1 minute.

4. Remove the hake and vegetable julienne from the liquid and set aside. Boil the liquid vigorously until it is reduced by about two-thirds, then season with salt and black pepper and leave to cool.

5. Heat the oven to 400°F/200°C/gas mark 6 and lightly grease a baking sheet. Roll out the pastry to a thickness of about $\frac{1}{4}$ inch (6 mm) and cut out $1\frac{1}{2}$ inch (4 cm) squares. Place the pastry squares on the baking sheet, brush with milk and bake in the oven for 4–5 minutes, until the puffs have risen and are light golden brown in colour. Remove the puffs from the oven and place on a wire rack to cool.

6. With a knife, remove and discard the top layer of each puff. Make a small incision in the pastry to separate the layers and form a hollow. Spoon as much hake filling into each puff as possible, otherwise the flavour will be lost in the pastry. Place the puffs on a greased baking sheet and warm through in a 350°F/180°C/gas mark 4 oven for 3–4 minutes before serving.

Note: You can bake the puffs a day ahead if you wish. Store them in an airtight container overnight.

Hake Puffs.

MONKFISH PIZZARETTES

Chunky monkfish and a colourful sauce make these miniature pizzas very moreish. Making your own dough may seem time-consuming, but it is fun to do and well worth the effort.

SERVES 15

INGREDIENTS
2 tablespoons olive oil
1 lb (450 g) monkfish fillet, cut
    into 30 cubes
3 shallots, finely chopped
3 tablespoons brandy
1 tablespoon white wine
1 tablespoon tomato paste
1 tablespoon chopped parsley
salt
freshly ground black pepper

FOR THE PIZZA DOUGH
$\frac{1}{2}$ tablespoon caster sugar
$\frac{1}{2}$ pint (300 ml) tepid water
$\frac{1}{2}$ oz (15 g) dried yeast
1 lb (450 g) strong white plain
    flour
1 tablespoon olive oil
a little olive oil for brushing

1. First make the pizza dough. In a cup, dissolve the sugar in the water. Sprinkle in the yeast, stir and leave in a warm place for 5 minutes, until the yeast has completely dissolved and the liquid is slightly frothy.

2. Sift the flour and salt into a large bowl, then pour in the yeast liquid and olive oil. Mix to a stiff dough, then turn out on to a floured surface and knead for about 15 minutes – the dough will become elastic and much less sticky. Shape the dough into a ball and place it in an oiled bowl. Cover with a damp tea towel and leave in a warm place for $1\frac{1}{2}$–2 hours to prove – the dough should double in size.

3. Heat the oven to 425°F/220°C/gas mark 7 and oil a baking sheet. Punch down the dough, gather it into a ball and, on a well-floured surface, roll it into a circle about 18 inches (45 cm) in diameter. Using a $2\frac{3}{4}$ inch (7 cm) cutter, stamp out 30 rounds. Carefully lift them on to the baking sheet and brush each round with a little olive oil. Bake in the oven for 10 minutes – take care not to overcook or the dough will become biscuity.

4. Meanwhile, prepare the topping. Heat the oil in a pan and fry the fish over a medium heat for 2–3 minutes, then add the shallots and cook for a further 3 minutes. Pour over the brandy and ignite. Add the white wine, tomato paste and parsley, bring to the boil, then simmer for 5 minutes. Season with salt and black pepper.

5. Remove the fish cubes and from the pan using a slotted spoon place one on each pizzarette. Return the sauce to the boil and reduce slightly, to a coating consistency, then spoon a little over the cubes of monkfish. The pizzarettes are delicious eaten immediately or can be reheated in a 300°F/150°C/gas mark 2 oven for 5–8 minutes.

Note: The pizza dough can be made and cut into rounds in advance, then frozen until required. Cook from frozen in a 300°F/150°C/gas mark 2 oven for 20–25 minutes. If you are unable to get hold of monkfish, use another firm-textured white fish in this recipe – halibut or turbot would both be suitable. Fish such as these are robust enough to withstand a certain amount of waiting around and reheating without coming to too much harm. For an even simpler pizzarette, top the cooked dough rounds with a little chopped tomato, a sliver or two of anchovy and a slice of black olive and heat through in the oven for a couple of minutes.

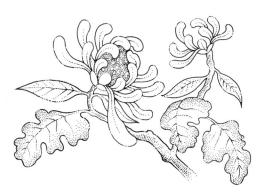

SALMON BROCHETTES *with* FRESH MINT

These brochettes offer a fresh combination of flavours – indeed, the fresher the raw ingredients, the finer the end result. They also benefit from the fact that they can be prepared mostly in advance and need only minutes of cooking before service.

SERVES 15

INGREDIENTS
1 lb (450 g) salmon, skinned,
    boned and cut into 1 inch
    (2.5 cm) cubes
1 sweet red pepper
1 sweet green pepper
1 sweet yellow pepper
olive oil for brushing

FOR THE MARINADE
1 tablespoon cornflour
1 teaspoon salt
1 tablespoon egg white, lightly
    beaten
30 leaves of fresh mint, finely
    chopped
ground black pepper for
    seasoning

1. Put 30 wooden cocktail sticks to soak in a bowl of water for about an hour. This will help prevent them from scorching when the brochettes are grilled.

2. Place the salmon in a bowl and sprinkle with the cornflour and salt. Pour over the egg white. With a fork, gently move the salmon around in the bowl to ensure that it is evenly coated. The fish cubes should absorb the flour, salt and egg white completely. Add the chopped mint, again making sure the fish is evenly coated, then place the bowl in the refrigerator for at least 30 minutes. Naturally, the longer the salmon is left to marinate, the stronger the mint flavour will be.

3. Meanwhile, skin the peppers using the technique described on page 52 (steps 1 and 2). Cut them into 1 inch (2.5 cm) squares.

4. Remove the salmon from the refrigerator and skewer each cube with one of the presoaked cocktail sticks. Skewer a square of red, yellow or green pepper on either side, so that the salmon is sandwiched between them.

5. Place the brochettes on a greased baking sheet, brush lightly with olive oil and sprinkle over some black pepper. Grill under a medium heat for 2 minutes, then turn them over and grill on the other side for a further minute. Transfer to a warm platter and serve immediately.

Note: The brochettes can be assembled 6–8 hours in advance and refrigerated, covered with cling film, until you are ready to grill and serve them.

RIGHT: *Prawn, Ginger and Spinach Omelettes (pages 28–29), Stuffed Baby Tomatoes (page 87)*

SQUID *in* SPICY TOMATO SAUCE

Even the squeamish will have no problem preparing this; the secret is not to overcook the squid, otherwise it toughens. The squid itself is very quick indeed, so if you are short of time forget about the sauce and serve it with wedges of lemon instead.

SERVES 15

INGREDIENTS
10–15 baby squid, about 1 lb
   (450 g)
plain flour for coating
olive oil for sautéing

FOR THE SAUCE
2 tablespoons olive oil
3 cloves garlic, crushed,
   1 medium onion
2 tablespoons tomato purée
2 × 14 oz (400 g) cans chopped
   tomatoes
$\frac{1}{2}$ pint (300 ml) red wine
1 tablespoon brown sugar
2 dried chilli peppers
1 tablespoon red wine vinegar
2 tablespoons finely chopped
parsley
salt
freshly ground black pepper

1. To make the sauce, heat the oil in a saucepan, add the garlic and onion, and sauté for about a minute, then add the tomato purée and cook for a further 30 seconds. Stir in the tomatoes, wine, sugar, chilli pepper, vinegar and parsley, bring the mixture to the boil, and simmer, covered, for 15 minutes, stirring occasionally. Remove the saucepan lid and allow the sauce to reduce for 30 minutes more.

2. Take the pan off the heat and purée the sauce by passing it through a sieve. Transfer the sauce back to the saucepan and taste to adjust seasoning – you will probably think it needs salt more than pepper. Set the sauce aside.

3. To prepare the squid, hold each one under a running cold tap and remove the head and tentacles with a slight tug. Discard these, unless you are fond of tentacles – they are much nicer than they sound. Peel away the skin from the main body (this will come away very easily), then turn the body inside out and clean away any remaining innards. Pat dry with kitchen paper.

4. Using a sharp knife, cut each cleaned body into rings of about $\frac{1}{4}$ inch (6 mm) thickness. Sprinkle some flour in a baking tray and draw each piece of squid through the flour to coat it, changing the flour whenever it starts to get sticky.

5. Sauté the squid rings in olive oil about 20 at a time, depending on the size of your frying pan, and drain them on kitchen paper as they are cooked – this only takes a minute or two. At the same time, gently reheat the sauce.

6. Pile the fried squid rings on a platter, then pour the sauce into a bowl and serve it alongside. Provide cocktail sticks so that your guests can pick up the pieces of squid and dip them in the sauce.

LEFT: *Bean Curd Puffs (page 68)*

WARM OYSTERS *in* COURGETTE WELLS

INGREDIENTS

20 medium-sized oysters
5 courgettes, about 5 inches
    (12.5 cm) long
6 tablespoons double cream
4 oz (100 g) cold unsalted butter,
    diced
1 tablespoon freshly squeezed
    lemon juice
salt
white pepper

For that special occasion or when you feel like pampering your guests, these are well worth the last-minute effort that is required in making the sauce. In fact, you will probably find that many of your guests prefer these warm oysters to raw ones. Allow two or three each as oyster-lovers are unlikely to be satisfied with less.

SERVES 8–10

1. Cut each courgette into four pieces each about 1 inch (2.5 cm) thick. Bring a saucepan of water to the boil and plunge in the courgette pieces. Boil for $1\frac{1}{2}$ minutes, then drain immediately and refresh under cold running water.

2. Pat the courgettes dry. Scoop out of each piece a hollow $\frac{1}{2}$–$\frac{3}{4}$ inch (1–1.5 cm) deep, using either a parisienne cutter or a teaspoon and being careful not to split the sides. Stand the hollowed-out pieces upside down on kitchen paper to drain.

3. Open the oysters, preferably with an oyster knife, working over a saucepan to catch their juice. Set the oysters aside in their shells.

4. Over a brisk heat, reduce the oyster liquid by two-thirds, then pass it through a fine sieve lined with muslin to remove any grit.

5. Bring the reduced oyster liquid to the boil in a clean saucepan. Add the cream and cook quite vigorously for 15–20 seconds to reduce it a little. If you cook it for longer than this, the cream will curdle.

6. Still over a high heat, thicken the sauce by whisking in $1\frac{3}{4}$ oz (45 g) of the butter. When the butter is incorporated, add the lemon juice and immediately remove the pan from the heat. Season with salt and white pepper, then whisk for a few moments off the heat.

7. Put the sauce into a clean, shallow saucepan over a low heat and add the shelled oysters, Swirling the pan in a circular motion, cook the oysters for about 30 seconds, until they are only just cooked through.

8. With a teaspoon, remove the oysters from the sauce one by one and place an oyster in each courgette well. Top up the wells with a little of the sauce, but don't fill them to the brim or they will be difficult for your guests to handle. Serve warm, and provide a small plate for each guest. It is advisable that guests drink the sauce before biting into the courgette, as the sauce is very runny and has occasionally even been known to spill on to shirt fronts.

Warm Oysters in Courgette Wells.

BEAN CURD PUFFS

Bean curd puffs, packaged in plastic bags, are sold in Chinese supermarkets, so at a pinch you can buy them already deep-fried for this recipe. However, you must recrisp them in the oven at 350°F/180°C/gas mark 4 for 10–15 minutes before filling the centres with the bacon and oyster stuffing. If the centres are not hollow enough, remove a little of the bean curd with a teaspoon before filling with the stuffing.

SERVES 8–10

INGREDIENTS

4 cakes bean curd, each about
2¼–2½ inches (6–6.5 cm) square,
drained
vegetable oil for deep frying
6 rashers streaky bacon
4 oz (100 g) can smoked oysters,
drained well and coarsely
chopped
freshly ground black pepper

1. Quarter each cake of bean curd and stand the pieces on two or three layers of kitchen paper to absorb excess moisture.

2. Half fill a wok with vegetable oil and heat to 400°F (200°C). Carefully place the bean curd into the oil and deep-fry for 13–15 minutes, until they are golden brown and the centres become almost hollow. They will float as soon as they are ready. If the bean curd appears to be colouring too quickly, reduce the heat and continue frying. Move the pieces around occasionally, using either a pair of chopsticks or a perforated spoon, if they appear to be sticking together. Remove from the oil using a large hand strainer or slotted spoon, and drain on kitchen paper. Leave to cool for about 10 minutes.

3. Grill the bacon well on both sides. When it is cool, chop it finely into a bowl, add the smoked oysters and some black pepper, and mix well together.

4. Cut the bean curd cubes into halves, and fill the centres with a teaspoon or two of the bacon and oyster mixture. Decorate them with some chopped parsley and serve at room temperature. If preferred, they can be warmed up under the grill for 30–60 seconds.

Note: The deep-fried bean curd cubes will remain moist if kept covered, in the refrigerator, for 2–3 days.

CRÈME FRAÎCHE PIROSHKIS

INGREDIENTS

1 tablespoon butter
1 onion, finely chopped
8 oz (225 g) lean minced beef
1 hard-boiled egg, finely chopped
1 tablespoon finely chopped fresh
     dill
salt
freshly ground black pepper
1 egg lightly beaten with 1
     tablespoon water

FOR THE PASTRY

7 oz (200 g) plain flour
$\frac{1}{2}$ teaspoon baking powder
$\frac{1}{2}$ teaspoon salt
4 oz (100 g) unsalted butter,
     chilled and cut into small
     pieces
4 oz (100 g) crème fraîche
1 egg, lightly beaten

I was taught how to make these delicious savouries while at university, by a language student who had spent 6 months in Russia. Without fail, he would make a batch every Sunday afternoon for snacks during his studies in the week ahead. But the batch never lasted longer than two days as his house-mates would invariably sneak them from the refrigerator.

SERVES 15–20

1. First prepare the pastry. Sift the flour, baking powder and salt into a bowl so that they are thoroughly mixed. Add the pieces of butter, tip into the bowl of a food processor and process until the mixture resembles coarse breadcrumbs. Add the crème fraîche and egg, and process for about 20 seconds, until the ingredients are well blended. Remove the dough from the food processor and knead on a lightly floured surface for about a minute. Form the dough into a ball, wrap it in cling film and refrigerate for 1–2 hours.

2. Meanwhile, make the filling. In a medium-sized heavy-bottomed saucepan, melt the butter over a moderate heat. Add the onion and sauté until soft but not browned, stirring frequently. Add the meat and, breaking it up with a fork, cook until browned and crumbly. Remove the pan from the heat and mix in the hard-boiled egg, dill, salt and pepper.

3. On a lightly floured surface, roll out the pastry to $\frac{1}{8}$ inch (3 mm) thickness and cut out rounds using a 3 inch (7.5 cm) pastry cutter. Place a teaspoon of filling in the centre of one half of each pastry round. Brush the edges with a little of the egg and water mixture, and fold the pastry over to make a half moon, pressing the edges together to seal.

4. Heat the oven to 400°F/200°C/gas mark 6 and lightly grease and flour a baking sheet. Arrange the piroshkis, spaced slightly apart, on the baking sheet, brush them with egg and water, and prick the top of each with a fork. Bake in the oven 15–20 minutes, or until golden brown. Serve warm.

MEATBALLS *with* PRESERVED TANGERINE PEEL

When it comes to meatballs, the Chinese have a penchant for a smooth texture that will roll along the palate. These meatballs, with their subtle yet distinctive preserved tangerine flavour, aim to achieve just that. Tangerine peels are preserved by being exposed to the sun intermittently until they are brittle. Like good wine, age improves their aroma. Xinhui, a small county not far away from Canton, produces top-quality peels and they are available in Chinese supermarkets. Orange peels are no substitute, and should not be used in their place.

SERVES 15

INGREDIENTS

2 large pieces preserved tangerine peel
1 lb (450 g) beef, top rump or skirt
$\frac{3}{4}$ teaspoon salt
$\frac{1}{2}$ teaspoon sugar
1$\frac{1}{2}$ tablespoons thick or dark soy sauce
freshly ground black pepper
1 teaspoon ginger juice (see page 13)
2 teaspoons Shaoxing wine or medium dry sherry
2 teaspoons potato flour or arrowroot
4 tablespoons water
10 canned water chestnuts, drained and minced in a food processor or very finely chopped by hand
3$\frac{1}{2}$–4 fl oz (100–120 ml) groundnut or vegetable oil
1 tablespoon sesame oil
4 large cloves garlic, crushed
sweet chilli sauce as a dipping sauce

1. Soak the tangerine peels in cold or warm water for 3–4 hours until they are soft, then drain well. Using a small knife, scrape off and discard the slightly bitter layer on the inside of the peels, then chop them very finely. You should have about 2 tablespoons of chopped peel.

2. Mince the beef very finely in a food processor until it is almost puréed. Transfer to a large bowl.

3. Add the salt, sugar, soy sauce, pepper, ginger juice, wine or sherry and potato flour or arrowroot to the beef and stir to mix thoroughly. Add the water, a tablespoon at a time, and stir-beat vigorously in one direction until smooth between each addition. Add the water chestnuts and tangerine peel and stir until totally incorporated. Stir in 1$\frac{1}{2}$ tablespoons of the groundnut or vegetable oil and the sesame oil, mixing well.

4. Scoop up 1–1$\frac{1}{2}$ teaspoons of the mixture at a time and roll it lightly between your palms for a few seconds to form a ball. The beef should not be sticky on your palms if it has been properly stirred. If it is, smear your palms with a film of oil. You should be able to make 50–75 meatballs.

5. Heat a deep, straight-sided sauté pan or a large, heavy frying pan over a high heat until very hot. Add half of the remaining oil, making sure it covers the whole surface of the pan, and heat until hot. Add half the garlic and fry until very brown, then remove the garlic from the pan and discard.

6. Reduce the heat. One by one, add half of the meatballs and brown them. Turn them over, one by one, and continue to brown and cook for about 3 minutes, or until just done. Remove to a serving dish. Wash and dry the pan, then reheat and use the remaining oil and garlic to fry the remaining meatballs in the same way.

7. Serve warm with sweet chilli sauce as an optional dipping sauce. Interestingly, rather than detracting from the flavour, a small smear of the chilli sauce draws out the aroma of the tangerine peel. Provide cocktail sticks for your guests to skewer the meatballs with.

BRIOCHES *with* SWEETBREADS

This recipe for brioche works for us every time. It is more straightforward and easier than other recipes for a similar dough and I would recommend it to any party host or hostess. The brioches have an excellent texture and buttery flavour that is more than appropriate with these Italian-style sweetbreads.

SERVES 15

INGREDIENTS

1 oz (25 g) butter for sautéing
8 oz (225 g) veal sweetbreads, cut into small thin slices
4 rashers bacon, finely diced
3 fl oz (90 ml) Marsala
3 fl oz (90 ml) double cream
salt
freshly ground black pepper
1 tablespoon finely chopped parsley

FOR THE BRIOCHE DOUGH

1 oz (25 g) sugar
2 fl oz (60 ml) tepid water
½ oz (15 g) dried yeast
5 eggs
1 lb (450 g) strong plain flour
large pinch of salt
6 oz (175 g) butter, cut into small pieces

1. Make the brioche dough a day ahead. In a cup, dissolve the sugar in the water, then sprinkle in the yeast. Stir and leave in a warm place for 5 minutes, until the yeast has completely dissolved and the liquid is slightly frothy.

2. Beat 4 of the eggs into the yeasty liquid, then beat in the flour and salt to form a dough. Hand-held electric beaters are very good for this task. When the mixture is smooth, gradually beat in the butter – when all of the butter has been added, the dough should have a silky appearance. You may also find it is a little wet, but that is how it should be. Put the dough in a polythene bag and leave it to rest in the refrigerator overnight.

3. Grease 30–36 individual brioche moulds or small fluted tartlet tins. Remove the dough from the refrigerator and weigh it into 1 oz (25 g) portions. Roll these into balls, then place in the prepared moulds. Press a small well in the centre of each ball with your thumb. Beat the remaining egg, and use it to brush the brioches lightly. Set the remaining beaten egg aside. Cover the brioches with cling film and leave to prove in a warm place until the dough has doubled in size – this will take about an hour.

4. Heat the oven to 425°F/220°C/gas mark 7. Brush the brioches again with the remaining beaten egg, then bake in the oven for 20 minutes, until light golden brown in colour. Remove from the moulds with a sharp-pointed knife and place on a wire rack.

5. To make the filling, melt the butter in a heavy-bottomed saucepan and add the sweetbreads and bacon. Sauté for 3 minutes, then add the Marsala and deglaze the pan. Cook for a further 2 minutes. Add the cream, salt and pepper, reduce the heat and cook for 2 minutes more.

6. Cut the brioches open near the top, being careful not to cut them through completely. Spoon about 2 teaspoons of filling into each brioche and sprinkle some finely chopped parsley over the filling to prevent it from looking bland. There will be no need to reheat the brioches before serving, provided that they were baked within the past hour. If not, they can be warmed through for 4 minutes in a 300°F/150°C/gas mark 2 oven. Arrange the warm brioches on a platter, allowing two for each guest.

Note: For a vegetarian version of this recipe, a filling of grated cheese works very well. Choose a tangy herb cheese, such as Cotswold, which provides a nice contrast to the brioche. Add the filling as described above, and warm for 4 minutes in a 300°F/150°C/gas mark 2 oven before serving.

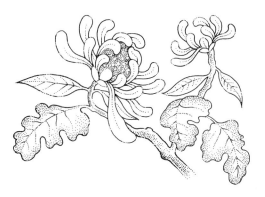

HALF-MOON WONTONS

So universally popular are wontons that the word itself is listed in English dictionaries. They are Chinese dumplings with paper-thin wrappers – skins – made from wheat flour and egg. There are regional variations, differing in shape and filling ingredients. These half-moon ones are my own version, Cantonese in origin, and filled with minced pork and prawn. They are served in a light sauce instead of soup so that they are suitable as cocktail food. In the same family are deep-fried wontons (see page 98), albeit prepared in a very different way, except for the skins.

SERVES 25–30

INGREDIENTS

8 medium-sized dried Chinese mushrooms, reconstituted (see page 13)
4 oz (100 g) drained canned bamboo shoots
6 oz (175 g) medium-sized raw prawns in the shell but without heads
13 oz (375 g) well-trimmed lean pork, minced
3 oz (75 g) pork fat, finely minced
1 teaspoon salt
½ teaspoon sugar
2 tablespoons thin or light soy sauce
1 tablespoon Shaoxing wine or medium-dry sherry
freshly ground black pepper
1 teaspoon potato flour or arrowroot
3 tablespoons water
8–12 spring onions, trimmed, halved lengthways then cut into tiny rounds
1 tablespoon sesame oil
1 large egg yolk
80–90 wonton skins, each about 3 inch (7.5 cm) square
80–90 coriander or watercress leaves
vegetable oil for cooking

FOR THE SAUCE:
3 tablespoons groundnut or vegetable oil
1 tablespoon sesame oil
6 tablespoons thin or light soy sauce
2 tablespoons water
freshly ground black pepper
hot oil to taste (optional)

1. Drain the Chinese mushrooms. Cut into very thin strips then into small dice.

2. Blanch the bamboo shoots in boiling water for 30–45 seconds to rid them of any canning odour. Refresh under cold running water and pat dry. Finely chop the bamboo shoots, either by hand or in a food processor. If using the latter, it is advisable to pulse to avoid making them mushy.

3. Shell the prawns. Halve them lengthways, removing the black veins, cut into small dice.

4. Put the pork and pork fat in a large bowl and mix in the prawns. Add the salt, sugar, soy sauce, wine or sherry, pepper and potato flour, then add the water, a tablespoon at a time, stirring vigorously until absorbed between each addition.

5. Pick up the pork mixture with one or both hands and throw it back into the bowl. Repeat this hard throwing action about a hundred times, so that the final texture will be both light and crisp.

6. Add the mushrooms, bamboo shoots and spring onions to the pork mixture and mix well. You may prefer to use your clean hands to do this. Leave to stand for about 20 minutes, then blend in the sesame oil.

7. When you are ready to wrap the wontons, stir the egg yolk into the stuffing. This will bind the stuffing to the skins. Pick up five or six wonton skins, or however many you can handle at a

time, and cut off the four corners using a pair of scissors, making the skins circular in shape. Trim all the skins in a similar way.

8. Place a skin on the palm of your hand. Place a coriander or watercress leaf just off centre on the skin. Put a heaped teaspoon of stuffing on the leaf, pressing it into an oblong shape. Pick up the skin flap near yourself and fold it over the stuffing to meet the opposite flap. Pinch tightly around the edges of the stuffing, making a few creases as well – this way the wonton will not fly open while being boiled. Put the wonton on a tray, and repeat until all the stuffing is used up. There is no need to flour the tray. Cover the wontons with a dry cloth as you go along.

9. Heat the groundnut or vegetable oil for the sauce in a small saucepan until smoke rises. Remove the pan from the heat and add the sesame oil. Allow to cool for 10 minutes or longer. Put the soy sauce and water in a small bowl and gently beat in the oil until amalgamated. Add some black pepper and the hot oil, if you are using it.

10. To cook the wontons, more than half fill a wok or large saucepan with water. Bring to a rolling boil, and pour in 1–2 tablespoons of vegetable oil. Add 20–30 wontons to the wok and return the water to the boil. Continue to boil, uncovered, for about 4 minutes, or until the wontons are cooked and floating to the surface with their skins translucent. Remove the wontons from the wok using a large hand strainer or slotted spoon and keep warm in a serving dish. Cook the remaining wontons in the same way. If the water looks murky, throw it away and use fresh water.

11. Serve the wontons warm. Pour several tablespoons of the sauce on to each dish of wontons, and let your guests pick them up with cocktail sticks or bamboo forks. Provide your guests with paper napkins to catch the sauce.

CHAR SIU TARTLETS

You have probably seen strips of roasted pork – char siu – hanging in the window of Chinese restaurants and have wondered how it is cooked. The answer is right here. Char siu makes a substantial dinner served with boiled rice and some greens. Cut up as a filling for pastry tartlets to go with drinks, it is equally delicious.

SERVES 20–25

INGREDIENTS

12 oz (350 g) plain flour
pinch of salt
9 oz (250 g) cold unsalted butter,
    cut into small cubes
4–5 tablespoons cold water
2½ lb (1.2 kg) shoulder or leg of
    pork
3 tablespoons runny honey
chopped coriander leaves, for
    garnish

FOR THE MARINADE
1 teaspoon salt
4 tablespoons sugar
4 tablespoons thin or light soy
    sauce
2 tablespoons hoisin sauce
2 tablespoons ground yellow bean
    sauce
1 tablespoon Shaoxing wine

1. To make the pastry, place the flour and salt in the bowl of a food processor, add the butter and process until the ingredients have the appearance of very fine crumbs. Gradually dribble in the water and continue to process until the mixture forms a loose dough. Do not add so much water that it becomes sticky. Remove the dough from the bowl and press it into a ball. Wrap in cling film and refrigerate for about 30 minutes.

2. Grease 50 circular tartlet tins about 1¼ inches (3 cm) in diameter. Cut the dough in half and roll out one half on a floured board until it is about ¼ inch (6 mm) thick. Moving it around at the same time, continue to roll the pastry until it is about ⅛ inch (3 mm) thick. Place a tartlet tin upside down on the pastry and cut around the tin, allowing a small margin. Cut out another 24 rounds from this sheet of pastry, then repeat with the remaining dough, making 50 pastry rounds in all. Press the pastry into the tins, making sure to fit it well into the base, and cut away excess pastry at the rim. Chill in the refrigerator for about 20 minutes.

3. Heat the oven to 375°F/190°C/gas mark 5. Bake the tartlets blind, either using baking beans or pressing an empty tartlet tin into the uncooked pastry shell, for about 10 minutes. Check that the tartlets are cooking evenly, then bake for a further 3–5 minutes. They should be a light golden colour. Remove the tartlets from the tins and leave to cool on a wire rack.

4. Meanwhile, prepare the char siu. Divide the pork into four strips, leaving on any fat because it is particularly delicious when roasted. Make three or four diagonal cuts in opposite directions, cutting about three-quarters of the way through the width of a strip without cutting it into pieces. This allows for better absorp-

tion of the marinade and gives the pork the traditional char siu look.

5. In a large bowl, mix together the salt, sugar, soy sauce, hoisin sauce, yellow bean sauce and wine or sherry. Put the pork into this marinade and leave for 4 hours, turning the strips every 30 minutes.

6. Heat the oven to 375°F/190°C/gas mark 5. Place the strips of pork side by side on a wire rack in the top third of the oven with a tray of water about $\frac{1}{2}$ inch (1.25 cm) deep underneath to catch the drippings. The steam from the water prevents the pork from drying up. Roast for 25–30 minutes, at the end of which time the top side of the meat will be reddish brown. Remove from the oven, dip each strip into the marinade and return to the rack with the underside up. Reduce the oven temperature to 350°F/180°C/gas mark 4 and continue to roast for another 25–30 minutes. Insert a skewer into the thickest part of a piece of pork: if no pink juices run out, the meat is cooked.

7. Remove the strips of pork from the oven and place them on a clean wire rack. Immediately brush all over with the honey, making sure to get into all of the crevices. Cut each piece of pork into four, then into small, thin slices.

8. Transfer the leftover marinade to a saucepan and reduce to a thick sauce. Remove the pan from the heat and combine with the carved pork. Leave to cool.

9. Using a teaspoon, scoop a small amount of the pork into each tartlet shell, then place them on a baking sheet. Reheat in a 350°F/180°C/gas mark 4 oven for 5 minutes and serve warm, garnished with some chopped coriander leaves. Let your guests pick up the tartlets with their fingers.

Note: The pastry shells can be cooked up to 3 days in advance and stored in an airtight container until required.

PHYLLO PASTRY PARCELS

There is an alternative, perhaps even more scrumptious way to cook these phyllo pastry parcels: deep-frying them. Simply put them in a wok half full of vegetable oil heated to 350°F (180°C) and deep-fry for 3–4 minutes, until they are golden and crisp.

SERVES 15–20

INGREDIENTS

8 oz (225 g) lean pork, minced in a food processor or very finely chopped by hand

1 oz (25 g) pork fat, minced in a food processor or very finely chopped by hand

¼ teaspoon salt

¼ teaspoon sugar

2 teaspoons thin or light soy sauce

1 teaspoon Shaoxing wine or medium-dry sherry

freshly ground black or white pepper

2 teaspoons finely grated ginger root

6 tablespoons water

1 oz (25 g) dried shrimps, rinsed, soaked in 2 teaspoons Shaoxing wine or medium-dry sherry, then minced in a food processor or very finely chopped by hand

10 canned water chestnuts, drained and minced in a food processor or very finely chopped by hand

2 tablespoons groundnut or vegetable oil

1½ tablespoons sesame oil

8 or 9 sheets phyllo pastry

vegetable oil for brushing

1. To prepare the stuffing, combine the pork and pork fat in a mixing bowl. Add the salt, sugar, soy sauce, wine or sherry, pepper and ginger, then add the water tablespoon by tablespoon, vigorously stir-beating after each addition. This has the effect of lightening the stuffing considerably. Add the dried shrimps and water chestnuts, stirring to incorporate them thoroughly. Stir in the oils until the mixture is smooth again.

2. Heat the oven to 400°F/200°C/gas mark 6 and lightly grease two or more baking sheets. Cut a sheet of phyllo pastry into three equal strips, each about 3½ inches (8 cm) wide. Lay out one strip on the work surface and very lightly brush with oil. Keep the remaining phyllo covered with a clean, damp cloth to prevent it from drying out. Put a teaspoon of stuffing on the lower left-hand corner of the oiled strip and fold the pastry over from that corner in the shape of a triangle. Fold over twice more, then cut the triangular parcel from the pastry using a sharp knife. Fold in the edges of the parcel to seal, brush with oil and place on a baking sheet. Use the remainder of the strip to make another parcel, discarding the leftover pastry trimmings. Repeat this process with the remaining phyllo until all the stuffing is used. Bake the parcels in the oven for 18–20 minutes, or until light golden brown in colour and crisp to the bite. Transfer to serving dishes and allow to cool slightly before serving.

Note: The stuffing can be made several hours in advance and stored, covered, in the refrigerator. The phyllo parcels can also be baked in advance and refrigerated or frozen, then reheated in a 400°F/200°C/gas mark 6 oven until thoroughly hot. This will take about 3 minutes if the parcels have been stored in the refrigerator, or about 6 minutes if they have been frozen.

How to make Phyllo Pastry Parcels.

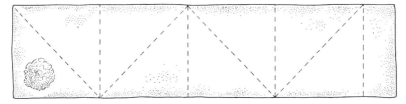

Lay out one strip of phyllo pastry and lightly brush with oil. Place a teaspoonful of the stuffing on the lower left-hand corner.

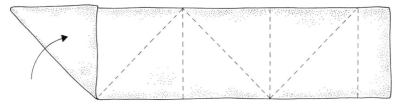

Fold the pastry over from that corner in the shape of a triangle.

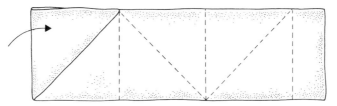

Fold over once more.

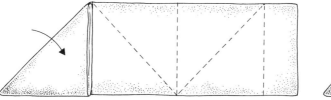

Fold over again, then cut the parcel from the pastry using a sharp knife. Fold in the edges of the parcel with oil and brush to seal. Use remainder of the strip to make another parcel.

FILLET STEAK *with* STROGANOFF DIP

The finest ingredients need only the simplest preparation. This party version of the classic stroganoff takes only minutes to prepare, and will be eaten just as quickly.

SERVES 15–20

INGREDIENTS
2 oz (50 g) butter
2 shallots, finely chopped
½ teaspoon Dijon mustard
¼ pint (150 ml) soured cream
salt
freshly ground black pepper
1 lb (450 g) fillet steak

1. Melt half of the butter in a pan and lightly fry the shallots until soft but not coloured. Remove the pan from the heat and stir in the mustard and soured cream. Reheat gently and season with salt and black pepper. Transfer the sauce to a bowl and keep warm in a bain marie.

2. Cut the steak into about forty ½–¾ inch (1–2 cm) cubes. Melt the remaining butter in a pan and fry the steak over a high heat for 2 minutes, moving it around constantly. The meat should remain deliciously rare.

3. As soon as the steak is ready, place the bowl containing the warm sauce in the centre of a large platter surrounded by the meat cubes. Serve with wooden skewers so that your guests can enjoy dipping the steak in the sauce.

RIGHT: *Half-Moon Wontons*
(*pages 74–75*)

SPARERIBS

INGREDIENTS
12 pork spareribs, about 2–2½ lb
 (900 g–1.2 kg)
about 2 tablespoons runny honey

FOR THE MARINADE
1 teaspoon salt
2 tablespoons sugar
3 tablespoons thin or light soy
 sauce
3 tablespoons hoisin sauce
1 tablespoon ground yellow bean
 sauce
2 tablespoons tomato ketchup
2 teaspoons Worcestershire sauce

Pork spareribs are such a deliciously desirable party food that it is worth one's while to serve them despite the inconvenience of the residual bones. Just pass around a large dish or two to take them off the hands of your guests.

SERVES 8

1. If a whole piece of spareribs is used, cut it up into single ribs then halve each rib crossways. This job is probably more efficiently done by your butcher, so get him to do it for you, if possible.

2. In a large bowl or dish, mix together the ingredients for the marinade. Add the spareribs, coating every piece evenly. Leave to stand for 2–4 hours, turning over the pieces every 30 minutes for better absorption.

3. Heat the oven to 400°F/200°C/gas mark 6. Place the spareribs on one or two oven racks in the top third of the oven with a tray of water ½ inch (1.25 cm) deep underneath to prevent the dripping juices from burning. If the gaps of the oven rack are too wide for the spareribs, place another wire rack on top crossways to form a grid. Roast the ribs in the oven for 15 minutes, at the end of which time the top side will be reddish brown. Turn the pieces over and baste them with the marinade. Reduce the oven temperature to 375°F/190°C/gas mark 5 and continue to roast for another 15 minutes. When the meat inside is opaque, the spareribs are cooked.

4. Remove the oven racks and place them on a heatproof surface. Using a cake brush, immediately brush the top side of every piece of sparerib with the honey. This glazing not only gives a sheen but also enhances the overall taste of the spareribs. Serve hot or at room temperature. They are even delicious cold!

LEFT: *Stuffed Chicory Leaves*
(*page 83*)

Water Chestnuts Wrapped *in* Bacon

INGREDIENTS
10–12 rashers streaky bacon
1 tablespoon runny honey
    dissolved in 1½ tablespoons hot
    water
2 × 6 oz (150 g) cans water
    chestnuts (20–24 water
    chestnuts), drained

There are usually one or two party eats on the menu that guests pick out as their favourites and watch for as the food comes around. This simple idea will be one of them. The thin honey solution provides its special flavour.

SERVES 10–12

1. Using a pastry brush, brush one side of each bacon rasher with the honey solution. Only brush one side, otherwise the bacon will be too sweet and sticky when eaten.

2. Cut each rasher in half widthways and wrap one piece of bacon around each chestnut. Place on a baking sheet, with the join underneath. Secure the bacon to the chestnuts with cocktail sticks if you wish, although these will turn brown during grilling.

3. Place the baking sheet under a hot grill and cook for 2–3 minutes. Turn the chestnuts over and grill for 2 minutes more. The bacon should be well cooked and slightly crispy – the more grilled the bacon, the greater the contrast in flavour between the bacon and the honey. If you have used cocktail sticks and they are rather scorched, it may be a good idea to remove them at this stage, before serving.

4. Transfer the chestnuts from the grill to a serving platter and serve immediately. Either provide cocktail sticks or bamboo forks, or let your guests use their fingers.

STUFFED CHICORY LEAVES

INGREDIENTS

1 lb (900 g) loin fillet of rabbit

1 tablespoon finely chopped shallots

30 tarragon leaves, finely chopped

3 tablespoons olive oil

6 tomatoes, skinned, seeded and chopped

12 mange-tout, cut into $\frac{1}{4}$ inch (5 mm) dice and blanched

2 sticks celery, cut into $\frac{1}{4}$ inch (5 mm) dice and blanched

2 carrots cut into $\frac{1}{4}$ inch (5 mm) dice and blanched

2 tablespoons dry white wine

3 heads of chicory

Very often with party food, the simpler the concept, the more impressed your guests will be. No one will deny that these leaves are both attractive and very, very tasty.

SERVES 15

1. Using a sharp knife, remove any membrane still attached to the rabbit. Cut each loin in half lengthways, then cut each half crossways into fine slices. Put into a small bowl and add the shallots and tarragon leaves. Pour over 2 tablespoons of the oil and leave to marinate for 30 minutes.

2. Heat a heavy-bottomed saucepan over a high heat and add the remaining olive oil. Quickly add the rabbit and cook, stirring constantly, for 2 minutes. Add the tomatoes, mange-tout, celery and carrots, and stir-fry for a further minute. Add the white wine to the pan and cook over a high heat until the liquid is almost completely absorbed. Remove the pan from the heat and leave to cool slightly.

3. Meanwhile, using a sharp knife, cut away the stem of the chicory, then cut off the larger leaves. Do not tear them off as the edges will become ragged and spoil the appearance. You will probably get 10–12 suitable leaves from each bulb. Wash the leaves and thoroughly pat dry.

4. Spoon about 2 teaspoons of the still-warm rabbit mixture into the hollow of each chicory leaf, at the end nearest the stem. Fill enough for two leaves per guest. Arrange the leaves on a large platter for guests to pick up with their fingers.

Note: The rabbit mixture can be prepared up to 24 hours in advance. Warm it through thoroughly in a saucepan before stuffing the leaves. If you do not like rabbit, chicken breasts could be substituted, following the preparation described above. However, once cooked, the chicken *must not* be reheated, and so should be served cold if prepared in advance.

SMOKED DUCK BREAST *and* APPLE STRUDEL

INGREDIENTS

1 tablespoon vegetable oil
2 cloves garlic, finely chopped
8 oz (225 g) eating apples, peeled, cored and diced
$\frac{1}{4}$ pint (150 ml) dry white wine
8 oz (225 g) carrots, peeled, finely grated and blanched
4 oz (100 g) frozen sliced French beans, thawed and drained well
6 sheets of phyllo pastry
2 oz (50 g) butter, melted
1 lb (450 g) smoked duck breast, cut into small thin strips

Strudel pastry is regarded as an art by most European chefs. However, this miniature savoury version of the normally sweet strudel does not require a great level of expertise to achieve excellent results.

SERVES 15

1. Heat the oil in a heavy-bottomed saucepan and cook the garlic until it is a light brown colour. Add the apples to the pan with the white wine, carrots and French beans, and cook over a medium heat for about 4 minutes – the vegetables should be only partially cooked.

2. Meanwhile, take a sheet of phyllo pastry and brush it with melted butter. On top of the melted butter lay another sheet of phyllo, brush again with butter and add a third sheet, then divide the stack of sheets lengthways in half. Repeat with the remaining sheets of phyllo. Cover the stacks of phyllo sheets with a clean, damp cloth so that they do not dry out.

3. Heat the oven to 375°F/190°C/gas mark 5 and grease a baking sheet. Add the smoked duck to the apple and vegetables, and stir to combine. The mixture should not be too wet – if it is, reduce it a little over a medium heat. Spoon a quarter of the mixture from the saucepan along the lower edge of the stack of phyllo sheets. Roll up into a long, tight tube, brush thoroughly with melted butter and place on the baking sheet. Make three more strudels in the same way. Bake for 15–20 minutes, until golden brown, then remove from the oven and transfer to a wire rack. When cool, cover and refrigerate until required.

4. When you are ready to serve the strudels, slice them into $\frac{3}{4}$ inch (2 cm) rounds. Place on a baking sheet and warm through for 5 minutes in a 375°F/190°C/gas mark 5 oven. Serve on a platter arranged in interleaved rows.

Note: The strudels may be kept in the refrigerator for up to 24 hours before they are sliced, warmed through and served.

CHICKEN WING STICKS

The recipe on page 100 tells you how to stuff the middle section of chicken wings, but you might wonder what could possibly be done with the upper section, or wing stick. I have therefore devised this recipe which, when not used at a drinks party, makes an appetising dish to serve with boiled rice.

SERVES 12–15

INGREDIENTS

24 chicken wing sticks
48 thin slices canned bamboo shoot, each about 1½ inch (4 cm) long
2–2½ tablespoons groundnut or vegetable oil
2 large cloves garlic, peeled and sliced
1 tablespoon Shaoxing wine or medium-dry sherry
½–1 tablespoon chilli sauce

FOR THE MARINADE

½ teaspoon salt
¼ teaspoon sugar
1 tablespoon thin or light soy sauce
1 teaspoon Shaoxing wine or medium-dry sherry
1 teaspoon potato flour or arrowroot
1 teaspoon sesame oil

1. First bone the wing sticks. Starting from the meaty end of a stick, simply cut through the skin and meat lengthways to the bone and scrape off the meat. Halve the meat lengthways and place it in a bowl. Repeat until all the wing sticks are done.

2. Add the salt, sugar, soy sauce wine or sherry and potato flour or arrowroot to the chicken, and stir to coat. Stir in the sesame oil and leave the chicken to marinate for about 20 minutes.

3. Meanwhile, blanch the bamboo shoots to get rid of any canning odour. Bring a saucepan of water to the boil, add the bamboo shoots and continue to cook for 30–45 seconds, then pour into a colander and refresh immediately under cold running water. Drain thoroughly.

4. Heat a wok over a high heat until smoke rises. Add the groundnut or vegetable oil and swirl it around, then add the garlic. As it takes on colour, add the chicken. Using a wok scoop or a metal spatula, toss and turn the chicken and garlic for about a minute, then splash in the wine around the sides of the wok. When the sizzling subsides, reduce the heat to medium, add the chilli sauce, stir to mix, then cover the wok and continue to cook for another 2–3 minutes, or until the meat becomes opaque. Scoop on to a dish with a slotted spoon.

5. Add the bamboo shoots to the wok and toss and turn until they have absorbed the sauce. Scoop them on to another dish.

6. To serve, place a piece of chicken, flesh side up, on each slice of bamboo shoot and skewer with a cocktail stick. Serve hot or at room temperature.

TURKEY BREAST, BLACK GRAPE *and* CURLY ENDIVE PITTAS

To make these eye-catching pittas even more of a talking point, you could use four wood pigeons, roasted for about 30 minutes, instead of the turkey breasts.

SERVES 10–20

INGREDIENTS
2 turkey breasts
about 2 oz (50 g) butter
3 tablespoons reduced stock
4 oz (100 g) black grapes, seeded
    and cut into quarters
Worcestershire sauce
1 small head curly endive,
    coarsely chopped
5 mini pittas
salt

1. Place the turkey breasts in a roasting tin with a good knob of butter on each one, and cover them with foil. Roast in a 400°F/200°C/gas mark 6 oven for 20–25 minutes, until cooked through. Allow the turkey breasts to cool slightly, then slice the meat into short, thin pieces.

2. Melt 1 oz (25 g) of butter in a saucepan over a low heat, then add the turkey and warm it through. Stir in the reduced stock and the grapes and continue to warm over a low heat for 2–3 minutes, until the grapes are slightly cooked. Add a few drops of Worcestershire sauce to heighten the flavour, and season with salt and pepper. Tip the endive into the pan then remove the pan from the heat. Leave to cool.

3. Cut the pittas into quarters and warm them under the grill for a minute or two. Spoon the turkey, grape and endive mixture into the pitta quarters and serve immediately.

STUFFED BABY TOMATOES

INGREDIENTS
30 cherry tomatoes, about 1 lb
    (450 g)
1 oz (25 g) butter
4 eggs, lightly beaten
2 tablespoons double cream
salt
freshly ground black pepper
3 teaspoons chopped parsley
1 tablespoon finely diced pickled
    cucumber
3 tablespoons grated Parmesan
    cheese

This is our variation on the ubiquitous stuffed tomato generally found at parties in the 1960s! The combination of pickled cucumber and scrambled egg is a perfect sweet-and-sour replacement for the scooped-out flesh of the tomato.

SERVES 15

1. Cut off and discard the tops of the tomatoes. Carefully scoop out the insides using the smallest scoop of a parisienne cutter, making sure that you do not split the bottoms and sides of the tomatoes.

2. Melt the butter in a saucepan, add the eggs and stir continuously for 1 minute. Add the cream and scramble together until only very lightly cooked. Season with salt and black pepper. Remove the pan from the heat and stir in the parsley, pickled cucumber and 1 tablespoon of the Parmesan cheese.

3. Using a teaspoon, fill each tomato with the egg mixture, forcing the mixture into the tomato with the back of the spoon. Sprinkle a little of the remaining Parmesan on the top of each tomato.

4. Stand the tomatoes on a baking sheet and place under a high grill for 30 seconds. Serve immediately on a warm platter.

COURGETTE *and* CHAUMES *on* PUMPERNICKEL

INGREDIENTS

6 oz (175 g) chaumes
8 oz (225 g) courgettes, finely
    grated
1½ oz (40 g) butter
salt
freshly ground black pepper
8 oz (225 g) pack pumpernickel
    cocktail rounds, or 8–12 oz
    (225 g–350 g) pumpernickel,
    cut into rounds with a 1½ inch
    (4 cm) pastry cutter
paprika, to decorate

Melted chaumes, flecked with buttery courgettes, makes a rich and generously flavoured companion for pumpernickel rounds. These canapés are delicious served warm, but the distinctive combination is almost as tasty eaten cold.

SERVES 15

1. Melt the butter in a saucepan over a medium heat and sauté the courgettes for 8–10 minutes, until soft.

2. Meanwhile, remove the rind from the chaumes, and use a sharp knife to dice the cheese as best you can. Set aside in a bowl until the courgettes are ready.

3. Add the courgettes to the chaumes and mix well with a fork, so that the heat of the courgettes melts the cheese. Season well. Using a knife, spread the mixture on to the pumpernickel rounds, and sprinkle lightly with paprika.

Note: If you plan to serve these canapés cold, add the paprika at the last minute. They will keep overnight in the refrigerator if necessary – again, add the paprika just before serving.

ARTICHOKE BOTTOMS *with* GOAT CHEESE

INGREDIENTS
3 × 4 oz cans (105 g cans)
  artichoke bottoms
4 tablespoons olive oil
12 oz (350 g) chèvre
1 clove garlic
3 sprigs fresh thyme
freshly ground black pepper
3 tablespoons crème fraîche
2 oz (50 g) fresh breadcrumbs
a little olive oil for baking
curly endive, to garnish

This is an easy, popular idea for a party canapé or a first course. The combination of goat cheese and artichoke makes a subtle yet substantial item for your party menu. The artichoke bottoms can be prepared ahead and quicky cooked just before they are needed.

Incidentally, artichoke bottoms are not the same as artichoke hearts, the bottoms are more tender. Most delicatessens stock them tinned.

SERVES 12

1. Drain the artichoke bottoms and rinse well under cold running water. Pat dry with kitchen paper. Put the olive oil in a bowl, add the artichokes and leave them to marinate for about an hour, turning at intervals – this will heighten their flavour.

2. Trim any rind from the chèvre and crush it in a small bowl with the garlic, using a fork. Add the chopped thyme, pepper and crème fraîche, and blend together.

3. Remove the artichoke bottoms from the oil and dab them dry, one at a time, on kitchen paper. Trim each bottom to sit flat and scoop out the insides to deepen the hollow, using a teaspoon or parisienne cutter. Spoon a mound of the chèvre mixture into the centre of each and stand them on a baking sheet.

4. Heat the oven to 375°F/190°C/gas mark 5. Sprinkle the chèvre with breadcrumbs and dribble olive oil over the top. Bake the artichoke bottoms in the oven for about 10 minutes, or until the crumbs are browned and the cheese is slightly melted. Garnish with curly endive, and serve warm, to be eaten in the fingers.

Note: You can stuff the artichoke bottoms several hours in advance. Simply top with breadcrumbs and a dribble of oil and brown in the oven just before serving.

Vegetable Tempura

INGREDIENTS

1 aubergine, cut into 1 inch
  (2.5 cm) cubes
¼ cauliflower, cut into bite-sized
  florets
1 sweet red pepper, seeded and
  cut into strips
4 oz (100 g) broccoli, cut into bite-
  sized florets
4 oz (100 g) okra, tops removed
4 oz (100 g) baby sweetcorn, tops
  removed, blanched for 3
  minutes
vegetable oil for deep-frying
1 tablespoon thin or light soy
  sauce
1 tablespoon Worcestershire
  sauce

FOR THE BATTER

1 large egg
4 fl oz (120 ml) water
4 oz (100 g) plain flour

The amount of vegetable preparation that can be done in advance makes this dish neither difficult nor time-consuming for a party menu. However, it is important that you make the batter at the last minute.

SERVES 15

1. To make the batter, break the egg into a bowl and beat lightly until foamy. Add the flour, then slowly add the water, continuing to mix until the batter is smooth.

2. Assemble the prepared vegetables on a tray near to a wok or deep-fat fryer. Ensure that all have been patted dry after washing or blanching.

3. Fill the wok or deep fryer one third full with vegetable oil and heat to 180°C (350°F). Dip a selection of vegetables into the batter, then carefully drop them into the oil. Do not overcrowd the pan. Deep-fry for about 2 minutes, until a light golden brown in colour, separating the pieces of vegetable with chopsticks. Remove from the wok or deep fryer with a slotted spoon, and drain on kitchen paper. Continue to fry the vegetables in batches until all are cooked, skimming the oil after each batch to remove loose pieces of batter.

4. Arrange the tempura on two platters. Sprinkle the soy sauce over one platter and Worcestershire sauce over the other and serve warm, accompanied by long, thin bamboo skewers.

TARTLETS of JERUSALEM ARTICHOKE PURÉE

INGREDIENTS
1 lb (450 g) Jerusalem artichokes
salt
freshly ground black pepper
3 oz (75 g) onion, chopped
butter for sautéing
5 tomatoes, skinned, seeded and
    chopped
tiny sprigs of parsley to garnish

For the puff pastry:
8 oz (225 g) plain flour
pinch of salt
6 oz (175 g) cold butter
1 teaspoon lemon juice
about 3 tablespoons cold water

The faintly sweet Jerusalem artichoke is neither an artichoke nor from Jerusalem; it is a member of the sunflower family, and originally from North America. No matter – these tartlets are ideal, subtly flavoured vegetarian drinks-party fare.

SERVES 15

1. First make the pastry. Sieve the flour and salt into a mixing bowl, then rub in 1 oz (25 g) of the butter until the mixture has the appearance of very fine crumbs. Make a well in the centre and add the lemon juice and sufficient cold water to make a soft, light dough. Turn out the dough on to a floured surface and knead until smooth, then roll into a rectangular shape. Mark the rectangle into three equal sections. Divide the remaining butter into three equal portions and place small pieces of the first portion on the bottom two-thirds of the pastry. Fold the top section over towards the middle section and then the bottom section over the other two sections. Turn the pastry round 90 degrees and roll back gently to its original rectangular shape. Repeat the process with the remaining two portions of butter, then wrap the pastry in cling film and place in the refrigerator until ready to use.

2. Peel the artichokes – you should have about 12 oz (350 g) after peeling – and boil in lightly salted water until tender. Purée in a food processor with a little black pepper and more salt if necessary (the salt will heighten the sweetness of the artichokes). Sauté the onions lightly in butter until a very light golden colour.

3. Heat the oven to 420°F/225°C/gas mark 7. Roll out the pastry to about $\frac{1}{8}$ inch (3 mm) thickness, then cut out circles to fit tiny $1\frac{1}{2}$ inch (4 cm) tartlet moulds. Spoon a small amount of the onion into each tartlet, followed by the artichoke and finally the tomato.

4. Bake in the oven at 420°F/225°C/gas mark 7 for 10–15 minutes, until a light brown colour. Decorate the tartlets with tiny sprigs of parsley and serve warm.

BRAISED CHINESE MUSHROOMS

In Chinese herbal medicine, these mushrooms possess the property of reducing blood pressure and stimulating the immune system. What more can we ask? While our tastebuds are being gratified, our health also benefits.

SERVES 12–15

INGREDIENTS

4 oz (100 g) thin mixed-size dried
  Chinese mushrooms,
  reconstituted (see page 13)
2 tablespoons groundnut or
  vegetable oil
1 tablespoon ginger juice (see page
  13)
1 teaspoon sugar
2½ tablespoons thick or dark soy
  sauce
1½–2 teaspoons sesame oil

1. Drain the Chinese mushrooms, reserving the soaking liquid. Leave the mushrooms damp and halve the very large ones.

2. Heat a wok over a high heat until smoke rises, then add the groundnut or vegetable oil and swirl it around. Tip in the mushrooms and stir for 20–30 seconds, so that the oil will give them fragrance while the moisture is absorbed.

3. Add the ginger juice and sugar. Stir rapidly for a couple of seconds, then add 4–5 fl oz (100–150 ml) of the mushroom liquid and the soy sauce. Bring to the boil, reduce the heat and continue to cook, covered, for about 15 minutes, or until the liquid has been absorbed. The mushrooms should be very tender by now. If any excess liquid remains, turn up the heat to reduce it.

4. Arrange the mushrooms, cap-side down, on one or two serving dishes. Using a small party brush, brush across the caps with the sesame oil. Serve either warm or cold, with toothpicks or bamboo forks. Your guests could also use their fingers.

VEGETABLE KEBABS

INGREDIENTS
4 oz (100 g) butter
6 fresh sprigs sage, finely chopped
salt
freshly ground black pepper
15 okra pods, about 3 inches
    (7.5 cm) long
10 baby sweetcorn
4 small leeks, thoroughly washed
    and cut into 1 inch (2.5 cm)
    pieces
2 sweet yellow peppers
15 firm cherry tomatoes, halved

*This is another idea that can be prepared a day in advance –
simply brush the kebabs with melted herb butter before cooking
and serving. It is well worth the trouble of preparing the herb
butter because it greatly increases the appeal of the kebabs.*

SERVES 15

1. Soak 30 thin bamboo skewers in water for about an hour.
This will help to prevent them from scorching when the kebabs
are grilled.

2. Soften the butter slightly, then blend in the sage, salt and
some black pepper. Set aside until you are ready to grill the
kebabs.

3. Blanch the okra in boiling water for 2 minutes. Drain and
refresh immediately under cold running water, then pat dry and
cut into 1½–2 inch (4–5 cm) pieces. Blanch the leeks in boiling
water for 1 minute. Drain and refresh immediately under cold
running water, then pat dry. Blanch the sweetcorn in boiling
water for 4 minutes. Drain and refresh immediately under cold
running water, then pat dry and cut into 1½–2 inch (4–5 cm)
pieces.

4. Skin the sweet peppers using the technique described on page
52 (steps 1 and 2). Cut them into 1 inch (2.5 cm) squares – you
will need 30 squares in all.

5. Assemble the okra, leeks, yellow peppers, cherry tomatoes
and sweetcorn on the bamboo skewers. Brush lightly with the
herb butter and place under a medium grill. Turn the kebabs
and brush again after 2 minutes, then again after a further 2
minutes. Grill for a final 2 minutes, then arrange the kebabs on
a large platter and serve warm.

BRAISED BAMBOO SHOOTS

INGREDIENTS

1½ lb (675 g) drained canned
  bamboo shoots
vegetable oil for deep-frying
1½–2 tablespoons sweet chilli
  sauce
1½–2 tablespoons thin or light soy
  sauce
⅓–½ teaspoon sugar
2–3 teaspoons Shaoxing wine or
  medium-dry sherry

Fresh bamboo shoots, a ubiquitous ingredient in things Chinese, are rarely if ever available in England so that we have no option but to resort to the canned product. Fortunately, the crisp texture, which is what bamboo shoots are all about, is not lost through the canning process. These wedges, deep-fried then finished in a light chilli sauce, never go begging at a party.

SERVES 12–15

1. Cut the bamboo shoots into bite-sized wedges, then blanch them in boiling water for 30–60 seconds to restore them to their best natural taste. Drain and refresh under cold running water, then pat dry on kitchen paper.

2. Half fill a wok or deep-fryer with oil. Heat to a temperature of 375°F (190°C), then carefully add the bamboo shoots and deep-fry for 1½–2 minutes, or until just the edges have turned brownish. Remove from the oil using a hand strainer or large perforated spoon and spread out on to kitchen paper to absorb excess oil. Empty all but about 1 tablespoon of the oil from the wok into a container and save for use on another occasion.

3. In a small bowl, mix together the chilli sauce, soy sauce and sugar and put nearby.

4. Reheat the oil in the wok over a high heat. When hot, return the bamboo shoots to the wok and stir until heated through. Add the wine or sherry around the edges of the wok and, when the sizzling subsides, pour in the sauce. Reduce the heat to medium and continue to stir, coating the bamboo shoots with the sauce for about another minute, or until the sauce is absorbed. Remove to a serving dish and serve hot or warm.

Note: These bamboo shoots are even delicious served cold, so may be prepared several hours in advance.

STUFFED BUTTON MUSHROOMS

INGREDIENTS

8 oz (225 g) drained canned
    bamboo shoots
4 oz (100 g) drained brine-packed
    green olives
$\frac{1}{2}$ teaspoon salt
5 tablespoons olive oil
4–6 spring onions, trimmed and
    chopped into tiny rounds
$1\frac{1}{2}$ lb (675 g) fresh button
    mushrooms, about $1\frac{1}{2}$ inch
    (4 cm) in diameter

Stuffed mushrooms per se are common enough at cocktail parties; what is alluring about these ones is the stuffing. By combining the Chinese bamboo shoots and spring onions with the Mediterranean olives, we have created a quartet of harmonising tastes and contrasting textures. The mushrooms are very easy to prepare, and can be served hot, warm or even cold – an extra bonus.

SERVES 15–20

1. Blanch the bamboo shoots in boiling water for about 20 seconds, then refresh under cold running water, to remove any canning odour. Mince them in a food processor or chop very finely by hand. Put the bamboo shoots in a mixing bowl.

2. Mince or chop the olives and add them to the bamboo shoots. Add the salt and mix well.

3. Heat a wok over a high heat until smoke rises. Add 4 table-spoons of the olive oil and swirl it around. Add the spring onions and stir a few times to season the oil. Tip in the bamboo shoots and olives, and stir rapidly for a few seconds. Reduce the heat to medium, continuing to stir until the ingredients are thoroughly hot, then scoop the stuffing mixture on to a dish and allow to cool.

4. Brush a large baking sheet with the remaining olive oil. Wash and pat dry the mushrooms, and carefully remove the stalks (these can be put into the stockpot). Using a small spoon, fill each mushroom cap with $\frac{1}{2}$–$\frac{3}{4}$ teaspoon of stuffing, piling it on to make a small mound. Line them up on the baking sheet.

5. Place the baking sheet under a very hot grill for 5–7 minutes, or until the mushrooms are cooked but not limp. Arrange the mushrooms on a serving dish for your guests to pick up with their fingers.

Note: The stuffing can be prepared several hours in advance.

RIGHT: *Chicken Wing Sticks*
(*page 85*)
OVERLEAF: *Wriggling Prawns*
(*page 113*)

DEEP-FRIED PARTY EATS

SWEET *and* SOUR WONTONS

These flowerlike wonton parcels are a favourite Cantonese snack, the more delicious if the sweet and sour sauce is imaginative rather than cloying and gluey. Using caramelised sugar, you will find that the sauce is not only richer in taste but also has a colour that is pleasing without having to resort to food colouring.

SERVES 15

INGREDIENTS

25 small raw prawns, in the shell but without heads, or 50 small cooked shrimps
50 wonton skins, each about 3 inch (7.5 cm) square
1 egg white, lightly beaten
vegetable oil for deep-frying

FOR THE SWEET AND SOUR SAUCE
$\frac{3}{4}$ pint (450 ml) water
7 tablespoons sugar
1 teaspoon salt
2 teaspoons thin or light soy sauce
3 tablespoons sweet tomato ketchup
4 tablespoons Chinese rice vinegar or 3 tablespoons white wine vinegar
1 tablespoon potato flour or arrowroot dissolved in 2–3 tablespoons water

1. First prepare the sweet and sour sauce. Put the water in a jug and leave nearby – it is essential to have the water at hand. Heat a heavy-bottomed medium-sized saucepan over a high heat for a few seconds, then add the sugar, the bottom layer of which will start to melt and turn brown almost instantly. Lift the pan and hold it just above the heat, then continue to melt the sugar, tipping the pan towards one side, then the other, for even melting. When the sugar has turned into a nut brown syrupy caramel but before it gets too dark brown, pour in the water and replace the pan on the heat. A glassy piece of sugar will appear instantly in the water. Reduce the heat to medium and slowly bring the water to a simmer, melting the glassy sugar completely. Add the salt, soy sauce, tomato ketchup and vinegar. Stir the potato flour or arrowroot mixture thoroughly, then pour it into the saucepan in a thin stream, stirring continuously with a wooden spoon to prevent lumpiness as the sauce thickens. Remove the pan from the heat and pour the sauce into one or two serving bowls. Set aside to cool.

2. If frozen raw prawns are used, thaw them thoroughly. Shell the prawns, remove the black veins and pat dry. Halve the prawns, ensuring that each cube is no more than $\frac{3}{4}$ inch (2 cm) long; otherwise you may have problems sealing the wontons. If cooked shrimps are used, trim to the right size as necessary.

3. Place a cube of raw prawn or a cooked shrimp on the centre of a wonton skin. Dip a finger into the egg white and draw a circle on the wrapper around the prawn or shrimp. Gather up the edges of wrapper and make a gentle twist, using the egg white to seal the wonton. Too hard a twist will result in a soggy bite in the middle when the wonton is deep-fried. Repeat until

all are done – making these wontons is a quick and easy job.

4. Half fill a wok or deep fryer with oil and heat to a temperature of 350°F (180°C). Tip in 10–15 wontons, or however many will float freely; they should expand almost immediately. Deep-fry for 30–45 seconds or until golden in colour. Remove with a hand strainer or large perforated spoon and drain on kitchen paper. Cook the remaining wontons in the same way.

5. Serve the wontons either warm or cold. Let your guests pick them up with their fingers, then dip them in the sweet and sour sauce. It is essential to provide paper napkins to catch any dripping sauce.

Note: The wontons will remain crisp for up to 6 hours, so they can be made in advance.

STUFFED CHICKEN WINGS

The unusual and delicious end result makes it well worth the effort of boning the wings. This may appear time-consuming and difficult, but you will soon get the knack and complete the boning easily. The wing tips can go in the stockpot, and the wing sticks can be used for another recipe (see page 85).

SERVES 10

INGREDIENTS
2 oz (50 g) drained canned
    bamboo shoots
24 chicken wings
2–3 oz (50–75 g) ham, thickly
    sliced and cut into strips about
    $\frac{1}{4}$ inch (5 mm) wide and 1 inch
    (2.5 cm) long
vegetable oil for deep-frying
sweet chilli sauce for dipping
    (optional)

FOR THE MARINADE
1$\frac{1}{2}$ teaspoons salt
2 tablespoons thin or light soy
    sauce
1 teaspoon honey
1 teaspoon Shaoxing wine or
    medium-dry sherry
1 teaspoon cornflour dissolved in
    1 teaspoon water
freshly ground black pepper

1. Slice the bamboo shoots fairly thickly. Blanch them in boiling water for about 20 seconds, then refresh under cold running water, to remove any canning odour. Cut into strips about $\frac{1}{4}$ inch (5 mm) wide and 1 inch (2.5 cm) long, and set aside.

2. To bone the wings, place a whole wing on a chopping board, find the joint between the wing tip and the middle section and slice through using a sharp knife. Sever the remaining joint, separating the wing stick from the middle section, and retain this middle section for boning. The aim is to remove the bone from the middle section of the wing without slitting the skin. Hold the section upright and using a sharp, pointed boning knife, work around the tendon and the larger and smaller bones, loosening the flesh. Hold on to the exposed bones with your fingertips and scrape the flesh downwards, turning the skin inside out. When you reach the end of the bones, cut them off from the flesh and discard them. The skin of the wing will now be inside out. Ease it back so that it is on the outside again. Repeat this boning procedure until all the wings are done.

3. Take a piece of ham and a piece of bamboo shoot and insert them into a boned wing. Fold any skin at the open ends inwards to form a parcel. Stuff the rest of the wings in the same way.

4. Put the salt, soy sauce, honey, Shaoxing wine or medium-dry sherry, cornflour mixture and black pepper in a large mixing bowl and stir well to combine. Add the wings and leave to marinate for about an hour. Turn the wings at least once during this time to ensure that they are evenly immersed.

5. Half fill a wok with oil and heat to 350°F (180°C). Meanwhile, remove the chicken wings from the marinade with a hand strainer or slotted spoon and let excess marinade drain off them. Carefully

add half of the chicken wings to the wok. The oil will froth up initially, then subside. Turn the wings intermittently with a pair of long chopsticks or a wooden spoon to ensure an even colour. Deep-fry for 4 minutes, until light brown and crispy, or until the chicken is thoroughly cooked. Remove from the wok using a large hand strainer or slotted spoon, and drain on kitchen paper. Reheat the oil to 350°F (180°C) and deep-fry the remaining wings.

6. Leave the wings to cool slightly, then serve as a finger eat, with a napkin. They are delicious on their own or with sweet chilli sauce as an accompanying dip.

SESAME PRAWN TOASTS

A very popular starter in Peking (Beijing) restaurants, these make excellent cocktail food. The secret lies in the technique of making the prawn paste, which is revealed below. Raw prawns must be used. If you can get them fresh, so much the better, but you are more likely to get frozen ones from Oriental supermarkets. As large prawns are very expensive, use the medium-sized ones which give you 30–40 to the pound (450 g).

SERVES 12–16

INGREDIENTS

1 lb (450 g) fresh or frozen medium-sized raw prawns, in the shell but without heads, thawed thoroughly if frozen

¾ teaspoon salt

2 teaspoons cornflour

1 egg white, lightly beaten

1½–2 oz (40–50 g) pork fat, minced in a food processor or very finely chopped by hand

8 canned water chestnuts, minced in a food processor or very finely chopped by hand

6–8 thin slices slightly stale white bread, crusts removed, about 3½ inch (8 cm) square

4 oz (100 g) white sesame seeds

vegetable oil for deep-frying

chilli sauce for dipping (optional)

1. Shell and devein the prawns. Pat dry, leaving them just damp, then mince in a food processor or chop very finely by hand. Transfer to a large bowl.

2. Add the salt to the prawn and stir in one direction until it is difficult to continue. Sprinkle with the cornflour, add the egg white and stir again vigorously for 1–2 minutes, or until the paste is light and fluffy. Add the pork fat and water chestnuts and stir to mix thoroughly. Refrigerate, covered, for at least 30 minutes.

3. Using a knife, spread the paste all over one side of each slice of bread. Leave the cut edges of the bread clean, but smear a tiny bit of paste over the corners to stick the paste to the bread. Spread the sesame seeds out on a dish and lightly press the prawn paste side of the bread on to them. Repeat until all the slices are done.

4. Half fill a wok or deep fryer with oil and heat over a high heat until it reaches 350°F (180°C). Add half of the pasted squares, paste side down, and deep-fry for about 1½ minutes, or until the corners take on colour. Turn over the squares and continue to deep-fry. As soon as the bread is golden brown, remove and drain on kitchen paper. Reheat the oil to 350°F (180°C) and deep-fry the remaining slices.

5. To serve, cut each slice into four strips, then halve each strip crossways, making eight bite-sized toasts from each slice. Arrange the toasts on a platter and serve hot with chilli sauce as an optional dip. Let your guests use their fingers to pick up the toasts.

SPRING ROLLS

The Chinese have been making these rolls in one form or another since the tenth century, the Song dynasty. In the twentieth century we can freeze them, and this is conducive to making a large quantity at a time. I have devised two sorts of cocktail-sized spring rolls, one vegetarian and the other with a small amount of pork to enrich the taste. If you wonder why bean sprouts, such an obvious choice of vegetable, are not included in either of the fillings, this is because their watery content is problematic for re-frying after freezing.

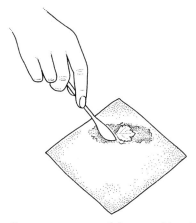

Put two teaspoons of the vegetable mixture just off centre on the corner nearest to you and place a coriander leaf on top.

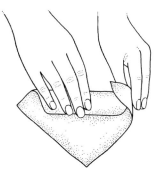

Fold the bottom flap over the stuffing, tucking the corner underneath. Roll up, folding the side flaps into the centre.

Brush the remaining flap with egg white.

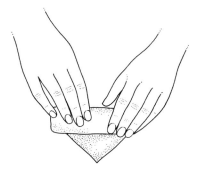

Fold over to seal.

(1) VEGETARIAN SPRING ROLLS

INGREDIENTS

10 oz (275 g) cellophane noodles
1 lb (450 g) carrots, finely
　shredded
5 sticks celery, cut into matchstick
　strips
15 dried Chinese mushrooms,
　reconstituted (see page 13)
4 tablespoons groundnut or
　vegetable oil
4 cloves garlic, finely chopped
½ inch (1.25 cm) fresh ginger root,
　finely chopped
8 oz (225 g) frozen, sliced french
　beans, defrosted and pat dried
1 teaspoon salt
3 tablespoons thin or light soy
　sauce
1 packet large spring roll
　wrappers, usually either about
　8 inch (20 cm) or 10 inch
　(25 cm) square, and about 25
　in a packet
about 100 coriander leaves
1 egg white, lightly beaten
vegetable oil for deep frying
Worcestershire sauce or chilli
　sauce for dipping

SERVES 25

1. Put the cellophane noodles into a large bowl and pour over 2 pints (1.2 litres) of boiling water. Cover and leave to soak and expand for at least 30 minutes. Drain well, then cut up roughly.

2. Blanch the carrots and celery separately in boiling water for about a minute. Drain and refresh immediately with cold running water. Pat dry to remove excess moisture.

3. Drain the mushrooms. Squeeze out excess water, but leave them damp. Shred into fine slivers.

4. Heat a wok over a high heat until smoke rises. Add the oil and swirl it around, then add the garlic and ginger. When the garlic takes on colour, add the carrots and celery, then the cellophane noodles, and stir for about a minute. Add the French beans and continue to stir-fry over a reduced heat until any excess water has evaporated. Season with the salt and soy sauce. Transfer the mixture to a dish and set aside to cool.

5. Place the spring roll wrappers in one pile on a flat surface and, using a sharp knife, cut the wrappers into four square piles. Put them into plastic bags to prevent them from drying up while you are making up the spring rolls.

6. Peel off a wrapper from one of the piles and place it on the work surface with a corner towards you. Put about 2 teaspoons of the vegetable mixture just off centre on the wrapper towards the corner nearest you and place a coriander leaf on top. Spread out the stuffing. Fold the bottom flap over the stuffing, tucking the corner underneath. Continue to roll, folding the side flaps into the centre so that they are incorporated in the roll. Leave no gaps in the roll as these would allow the filling to escape during deep frying. Brush the remaining flap with a little egg white and fold the roll over to seal. Repeat this process until the stuffing is used up.

7. Half fill a wok or deep-fryer with oil and heat to 350°F (180°C). Carefully slide 10–15 spring rolls into the wok or deep fryer and fry for 3–4 minutes, until a pale golden colour. Remove

from the oil and drain on kitchen paper. The spring rolls can be prepared up to this point several hours in advance.

8. To crisp the spring rolls, reheat the oil to 350°F (180°C) and deep fry them for a second time for about a minute, or until they are golden. To test for crispness, tap a spring roll with a chopstick. If it sounds hollow, it is ready. Remove the spring rolls from the oil and drain on kitchen paper. Serve hot, accompanied by Worcestershire sauce or chilli sauce as a dip. Fingers are the best implements to eat them with.

Note: For freezing purposes, the first deep-frying should be done 2–2½ minutes only, until the spring rolls are a pale ivory colour. They can then be frozen in the normal way inside freezer bags. In the second deep frying to crisp, heat the oil to 375°F (190°C), then carefully place the frozen rolls in the oil and deep-fry for about 4 minutes, until golden. This produces a very good result.

(II) PORK SPRING ROLLS

INGREDIENTS

8 oz (250 g) well trimmed lean
    pork, leg or shoulder
10–12 dried Chinese mushrooms,
    reconstituted (see page 13)
about 1½ lb (675 g) drained
    canned bamboo shoots, thinly
    sliced
3 tablespoons groundnut or
    vegetable oil
2 large cloves garlic, finely
    chopped
12 large spring onions, trimmed,
    cut into 1½ inch (4 cm) lengths,
    then finely shredded
1 tablespoon Shaoxing wine or
    medium-dry sherry
1 packet large spring roll
    wrappers, usually either about
    8 inches (20 cm) or 10 inches
    (25 cm) square, and about 25
    in a packet
Worcestershire sauce or chilli
    sauce for dipping

FOR THE MARINADE
¾ teaspoon salt
½ teaspoon sugar
1 tablespoon thin or light soy
    sauce
10 turns ground black peppermill
1 teaspoon Shaoxing wine or
    medium-dry sherry
1 teaspoon potato flour or
    arrowroot
2 teaspoons water
1½ teaspoons sesame oil

FOR THE SAUCE
1 teaspoon potato flour or
    arrowroot dissolved in 2
    tablespoons water
2 tablespoons thin or light soy
    sauce
¼ teaspoon sugar

SERVES 25

1. Cut the pork into paper thin slices about 1–1½ inch (2.5–4 cm) long. Pile several slices together at a time and cut lengthways into matchstick strips.

2. Put the salt, sugar, soy sauce, pepper, wine or sherry and the potato flour or arrowroot for the marinade in a bowl. Add the pork and mix to coat. Stir in the water, then the sesame oil. Leave to marinate for 20–30 minutes.

3. Drain the mushrooms, leaving them damp. Cut into paper thin slivers and set aside.

4. Blanch the bamboo shoots in boiling water for about 20 seconds, then refresh under cold running water, to remove any canning odour. Pile several slices of bamboo shoots together at a time and shred lengthways into matchstick sizes. Set aside.

5. To prepare the sauce, blend the soy sauce and sugar into the arrowroot mixture, and set aside.

6. Heat a wok over a high heat until smoke rises, then add 2 tablespoons of the groundnut or vegetable oil and swirl it around. Add the garlic and let it sizzle, then add half of the spring onions and stir for a few seconds. Add the pork and, going to the bottom of the wok with the wok scoop or a metal spatula turn and toss for about 1 minute, separating the strips. Splash in the wine or sherry around the side of the wok, continuing to stir and mix. When the sizzling dies down, reduce the heat down to medium and transfer the pork to a large bowl using a slotted spoon, so that any oil is left behind.

7. Add the remaining oil to the wok and swirl it around. Stir in the remaining spring onions, then the mushrooms, and then the bamboo shoots. Stir as you cook off any excess moisture. Stir the sauce thoroughly and pour it into the wok, then stir for about 30 seconds or until it thickens. The sauce seasons as well as binds the mixture. Remove the wok from the heat and scoop the mixture into a large bowl.

8. Mix the pork, mushrooms and bamboo shoots together. Leave to cool before you wrap the spring rolls. The stuffing should be moist.

9. Wrap, deep-fry and serve the spring rolls as for the Vegetarian Spring Rolls, steps 5–8 (page 104).

Note: Pork Spring Rolls may also be frozen. Follow the instructions given at the end of the Vegetarian Spring Rolls recipe on page 105.

SAVOURY CRISPY BEAN CURD

INGREDIENTS

4 cakes bean curd, each about
  2¼–2½ inches (6–6.5 cm) square,
  drained
vegetable oil for deep-frying
4 tablespoons cornflour
1¼ teaspoons spiced salt (see page
  13)
spiced salt for dipping
hot chilli sauce for dipping
  (optional)

In China, fresh bean curd cakes come in two consistencies – firm and soft. Abroad, in Britain and the United States for instance, bean curd comes more or less in one consistency, and that is on the firm-to-hard side. There is also a Japanese cartoned product with an extremely soft and silky consistency.

To make this recipe, neither the hard English nor the super-soft Japanese bean curd is ideal. The Chinese product sold in Chinese supermarkets should be used if possible.

Healthy as bean curd is, it is very bland in taste, so how do you transform it into an appetising cocktail party food that is also quite easy to make? The puzzle is unravelled in this recipe. Don't be put off by the deep-frying. It is done quickly and, at a pinch, the pieces can be recrisped in the oven. If you are also interested in sweet crispy bean curd, see the recipe on page 121.

SERVES 8–10

1. Quarter each cake of bean curd, then halve each piece widthways, making 32 cubes all together. Stand them on two or three layers of kitchen paper to absorb some of the excess moisture.

2. Half fill a wok or deep-fryer with oil and heat over a high heat until the oil reaches 375–400°F (190–200°C).

3. In the meantime, put the cornflour in a dish, add the spiced salt and mix thoroughly. Dip the bean curd, piece by piece, into the cornflour, turning it so that all the surfaces are covered. Discard the leftover cornflour.

4. Using wooden chopsticks or tongs, carefully place half the pieces of bean curd in the oil and deep-fry for 2–3 minutes, until they are pale golden in colour, the skin crisp but the inside still soft and curd-like. Gently move the bean curd around in the oil, separating any pieces that may have stuck together, after deep-frying for 1–1½ minutes. Remove from the oil with a large hand strainer or slotted spoon, and stand the pieces on kitchen paper to absorb excess oil.

5. Place a saucer of spiced salt and a saucer of hot chilli sauce in the centre of a large serving platter, and arrange the pieces of bean curd round them. Serve hot and let your guests use their fingers to pick up the pieces and dip them, sparingly, into the spiced salt for added savouriness. The chilli sauce is only for those who really like it hot!

Note: Even though it is not advisable to prepare the crispy bean curd in advance, pieces that have become cold and limp can nevertheless be recrisped in a 350°F/180°C/gas mark 4 oven for 5–7 minutes.

Taro Chips *with* Spiced Salt

INGREDIENTS
1 taro, about 2 lb (900 g)
vegetable oil for deep frying
1 teaspoon spiced salt (see page 13)

You will find taro in any Chinese supermarket or greengrocer that sells more exotic vegetables. It is a coarse-skinned root vegetable, rather like swede in appearance, which has a special, almost tangy flavour. These chips are especially good served with a glass of dry sherry.

SERVES 8–10

1. Peel the taro using a potato peeler or short-handled knife. The skin is usually very uneven so make sure you get into every crack. Cut the peeled taro into four even pieces and slice each quarter into fine slivers using a mandolin or hand grater with a slicing attachment. You will find that the taro becomes quite floury, but do not rinse it as this flouriness contributes to the unique flavour.

2. Half fill a wok with oil and heat to 375°F (190°C). Divide the taro slices into two batches and carefully put the first batch into the oil. Deep-fry for 3 minutes, separating the pieces at intervals using a pair of chopsticks or a perforated spoon. If the chips brown too quickly, reduce the heat and continue frying. Ideally they should be a light golden colour. Remove the chips from the oil using a large hand strainer or slotted spoon, and drain on kitchen paper. Reheat the oil to 375°F (190°C) and deep-fry for the second batch.

3. Meanwhile, sprinkle the first batch of chips with $\frac{1}{2}$ teaspoon of the spiced salt while they are still wet with oil, moving them around with chopsticks or a fork to ensure that they are evenly coated. When the second batch are cooked drain and season them in the same way. Serve the chips at room temperature.

Note: Taro chips are an excellent accompaniment for game in place of more traditional game chips. After slicing the taro, cut the rounds into strips and deep-fry for 2 minutes at 375°F (190°C). Season with spiced salt, as above.

MINT *and* BRIE GARBANZOS

INGREDIENTS

8 oz (225 g) chick peas or
   garbanzo beans, soaked
   overnight and drained
1 garlic clove, finely chopped
4 tablespoons chopped fresh mint
1 egg
salt
freshly ground black pepper
2 oz (50 g) brie, chilled
beaten egg and dry white
   breadcrumbs for coating
vegetable oil for deep frying

A crispy mint-flavoured coating encases melted brie in this different and delicious idea. Chick peas or garbanzo beans are becoming easier and easier to obtain, but the distinctive flavour and texture they provide is well worth any searching that may be necessary.

SERVES 15

1. Put the chick peas in a saucepan of fresh water, and boil briskly for 10 minutes. Cover the pan and simmer for 1–1¼ hours or until tender. Drain the chick peas, reserving 2 tablespoons of the cooking liquid.

2. In a food processor, purée the chick peas until smooth. Add the garlic, mint, egg and reserved cooking liquid, and blend well together.

3. Remove the rind from the brie and cut the cheese into 20 small cubes. Place a heaped tablespoon of the chick pea mixture in the palm of your hand, and flatten it into a small circle. Place a cube of brie in the centre, fold over the mixture to enclose the cheese completely, and shape into a ball about 1 inch (2.5 cm) in diameter. Repeat with the remaining cheese. Chill overnight in the refrigerator, if possible.

4. Coat each ball with egg and breadcrumbs. Half fill a wok or large saucepan with oil and heat to 350°F (180°C). Deep fry the balls for 2–3 minutes, until a light golden brown, and drain briefly on kitchen paper. Serve warm, to be eaten in the fingers.

Note: While it is not absolutely essential to chill these overnight before deep-frying, the end result will be more successful if you do.

SAVOURY CASHEW NUTS

INGREDIENTS
1 lb (450 g) shelled cashew nuts
vegetable oil for deep-frying
salt or spiced salt (see page 13)

For a drinks party, you can never go wrong by having some nuts around, and what can be better than cashew nuts? As they are expensive, it is worthwhile to make your own savoury crispy nuts. You can season the deep-fried nuts with either salt on its own or spiced salt – the latter undoubtedly adds an exotic quality.

SERVES 12–15

1. Blanch the nuts in boiling water for about a minute, then drain in a colander and refresh under cold running water. Dab dry excessive moisture with kitchen paper.

2. Half fill a wok or deep fryer with oil and add the nuts. Place over a high heat and deep-fry the nuts until they are light brown, or the oil temperature reaches 350–365°F (180–185°C). This will take about 8 minutes. While they are frying gently move the nuts around a couple of times with long chopsticks or a wooden spatula to make sure that those near the bottom do not get burned.

3. Remove the wok from the heat immediately. The nuts will continue to colour in the hot oil during the next 10 seconds, reaching the desired golden brown colour.

4. Using a large hand strainer, remove the nuts from the oil and place on a dish lined with greaseproof paper – rather than kitchen paper – to absorb excess oil. While they are still hot, sprinkle the nuts with salt or spiced salt (about 2–3 teaspoons). Mix well and leave to cool. Serve at room temperature.

Note: If kept in an airtight container, the nuts will not lose their crispness for up to a fortnight.

RIGHT: *Sweet and Sour Wontons (page 98)*

WRIGGLING PRAWNS

INGREDIENTS

1 lb (450 g) fresh or thoroughly
  thawed frozen medium-sized
  raw prawns, in their shells but
  without heads (about 25–30
  prawns)
¾ teaspoon salt
1½ teaspoons cornflour
1 tablespoon egg white, lightly
  beaten
vegetable oil for deep-frying

It is a treat to enjoy the taste of prawns alone, without the distraction of added sauces. As a rule, fresh prawns should be used as the Chinese emphasis is on raw ingredients – whether vegetables, poultry, meat or seafood – being fresh. But alas, we often have to bow to reality and resort to frozen raw prawns from China and other parts of the East or from Africa.

SERVES 10–15

1. Shell the prawns and pat dry. Stand them, one at a time, on a board or work surface and, using a sharp knife, halve them along the back, removing and discarding the black veins at the same time. Put the prawns into a large bowl.

2. Add the salt to the prawns and stir to mix thoroughly. Add the cornflour and egg white and stir again vigorously for 30–60 seconds until the cornflour and egg white have been absorbed. Refrigerate, covered, for about 6 hours or overnight. The marinating coupled with the chilling gives the prawns a light and crisp texture – what the Chinese look for when they bite into a prawn.

3. Half fill a wok with oil and heat over a high heat until it reaches a temperature of 350°F (180°C). Loosen the prawns in the bowl and, using a large hand strainer, gently add them to the oil. Deep-fry for 30–45 seconds, in which time they will be cooked. The prawns will curl up almost instantly when they are submerged in the oil. Move them about gently using a pair of long chopsticks or a wooden spoon to ensure even cooking.

4. With a large hand strainer or slotted spoon, scoop the prawns on to a large serving dish. Serve hot or warm and provide cocktail sticks or small bamboo forks, or just let your guests use their fingers.

LEFT: *Fruit Fondue with White and Dark Chocolate Sauces (page 117).*

SWEET POTATO CHIPS *with* AVOCADO *and* PRAWN DIP

INGREDIENTS

1 sweet potato, about 1 lb (450 g)
vegetable oil for deep-frying
4–5 teaspoons extra virgin olive
   oil
4 small spring onions, trimmed
   and chopped into tiny rounds
2 ripe avocados, peeled and
   stoned
1 teaspoon champagne or white
   wine vinegar
1½ tablespoons freshly squeezed
   lemon juice
½ teaspoon salt
6 oz (175 g) cooked prawns,
   coarsely chopped

If one experiments often enough in the kitchen, one is bound to come up with new and delicious ideas – or so one hopes. This recipe is the happy result of Paul and I working together with the intention of creating an East-meets-West eat: sweet potato and prawn meeting avocado and olive oil. We were so delighted with the end product that we polished off the whole bowl of dip and chips between us. I'm sure you will be more sensible and let your guests share it.

SERVES 10

1. Peel the sweet potato then slice it, using a mandolin or a hand grater with a slicer attached, into very thin rounds. Rinse the potato slices under cold water and pat dry.

2. Half fill a wok or deep fryer with oil and heat over a high heat to 375°F (190°C). Carefully drop the potato into the oil and separate the pieces with chopsticks or a perforated spoon. Continue to do this as you deep-fry them for 3 minutes. The chips should be light golden in colour. Remove the wok from the heat, and continue to fry for another minute. Remove the chips from the oil with a large hand strainer or slotted spoon and drain on kitchen paper.

3. To make the prawn and avocado dip, heat an empty wok over a high heat until smoke rises. Add 1½ teaspoons of the olive oil, heat until hot then toss in the spring onions, stirring them around constantly with a spatula for about 30 seconds so that they will release their flavour. Scoop the onions on to a dish and keep nearby.

4. Put the avocados into the bowl of a food processor and purée then, with the motor still running, dribble in the remaining olive oil. Add the vinegar and lemon juice in the same way. Do not over-process or the mixture may separate.

5. Transfer the purée to a bowl and add the salt, prawns and spring onions. Mix thoroughly, then cover and place in the refrigerator for 30 minutes to allow the flavour to develop.

6. Place the chips on a serving dish and serve accompanied by the avocado and prawn dip. Let your guests use their fingers to enjoy the dip with the chips.

Note: These chips can be made ahead if you prefer. Let them cool, then store in an airtight container. They will remain crisp for up to 2 days, and are good to eat even on their own. The dip can be made up to 6 hours in advance and stored, covered, in the refrigerator.

SWEET PARTY EATS

FRUIT FONDUE *with* WHITE *and* DARK CHOCOLATE SAUCES

INGREDIENTS
4 oz (100 g) seedless black grapes
4 oz (100 g) seedless green grapes
8 oz (225 g) strawberries
4 oz (100 g) kumquats
3 kiwi fruits
3 oranges
4 oz (100 g) dark chocolate
5 tablespoons crème fraîche
4 egg yolks
2 tablespoons fruit liqueur
4 oz (100 g) white chocolate

The simplest ideas can often be the most appealing. Guests will find this fondue refreshing after an evening of savoury canapés. Serve it when you would like your guests to leave as a sweet eat is a good clue that the party is over!

SERVES 15

1. Wash and dry the grapes, hull the strawberries, cut the kumquats in halves and peel and slice the kiwi fruits. Take a short, sharp knife and remove the peel and pith from the oranges then, working over a bowl, cut out the orange segments. Set the prepared fruits aside, reserving the juice in the bowl for adding to the sauces.

2. In a double boiler, melt the white chocolate. When it has melted, add 2 of the egg yolks and beat in thoroughly, then add 2 tablespoons of the crème fraîche and mix well. Stir in 1 tablespoon of the fruit liqueur – I find apricot brandy does very well – and 1 tablespoon of the reserved orange juice. Transfer the white chocolate sauce to a small ramekin, and leave to cool.

3. Wash out the double boiler and make the dark chocolate sauce in the same way but using 3 tablespoons of crème fraîche. If possible, use a different fruit liqueur this time. Transfer the sauce to a second ramekin and leave to cool.

4. Arrange the prepared fruits in clusters on a white platter with the ramekins of white and dark chocolate sauce either in the centre or alongside. Serve the fondue with wooden skewers or cocktail sticks.

APRICOT COLETTES

These apricot colettes will give an elegant finish to your party. The dark bitter chocolate shell contrasts in both colour and texture with the velvety apricot and toasted almond.

SERVES 15

INGREDIENTS
8 oz (225 g) bitter-sweet chocolate
4 oz (100 g) dried apricots, soaked
  overnight
1 oz (25 g) caster sugar
grated rind and juice of 1 orange
toasted flaked almonds, to
  decorate
30–40 petit four cases

1. Break the chocolate into pieces and melt it in a bowl over a pan of hot water. Using the handle of a teaspoon, coat the inside of the 30–40 waxed paper petit four cases with the chocolate. Leave to set in the refrigerator.

2. To make the filling, put the apricots and their soaking water in a saucepan with the sugar. There should be enough water to cover the fruit. Bring to the boil and simmer, uncovered, for about 25 minutes. The apricots should then be tender and the water reduced to a syrupy glaze.

3. Make the orange juice up to $\frac{1}{4}$ pint (150 ml) with cold water. In a blender, purée the apricots with the orange juice and grated rind, then set aside to cool.

4. Carefully peel off the paper from the chocolate cases. Fill each one with apricot purée, and decorate with toasted flaked almonds. Chill the colettes in the refrigerator until you are ready to serve them.

Note: The colettes will look just as attractive and taste just as good if they are made a day ahead and stored in the refrigerator.

MINT SPOONS *with* STRAWBERRY SAUCE

INGREDIENTS

8 oz (225 g) fresh strawberries, hulled
1½ tablespoons freshly squeezed lemon juice
1 tablespoon brandy
20 mint leaves
6 egg whites
9 oz (250 g) sugar
1 pint (600 ml) water
20 very tiny mint leaves to decorate

You would be advised not to attempt this recipe unless you have at least twenty dessert spoons available. They are the perfect and logical way to present this delicious strawberry and mint combination.

SERVES 20

1. Put the strawberries, and lemon juice and brandy into the bowl of a food processor and purée until smooth. Press the purée through a fine sieve into a small bowl, and place in the refrigerator to chill.

2. Blanch the 20 larger mint leaves in boiling water for about a minute, then drain and chop very finely.

3. Beat the egg whites in a mixing bowl, adding first the mint leaves, then the sugar, in a steady stream. Continue beating until stiff.

4. Fill a piping bag fitted with a large star nozzle with half of the egg white. Fold the sides of the bag over your hand and ensure that the mixture goes all of the way down to the bottom of the bag. Turn back the sides of the bag as you fill it. Pipe 10 rosettes about 1½ inches (4 cm) in diameter on to a sheet of greaseproof paper, then repeat the process with the remaining egg white, making 20 rosettes in all.

5. Pour the water into a large, shallow saucepan and set it over a medium heat. Bring to the boil, then reduce the heat so that the water simmers gently. Using a palette knife which has been dipped in hot water, carefully slide each rosette into the saucepan. Poach for 5 minutes, or until cooked through. Remove the rosettes from the saucepan using a slotted spoon and place on a clean sheet of greaseproof paper.

6. Put about a teaspoon of the chilled strawberry sauce in the bowl of each of 20 dessert spoons, and place a meringue rosette on top. Arrange the spoons on a circular tray with the handles jutting out from the edge, so that your guests can pick them up easily. Decorate each rosette with a tiny mint leaf.

RASPBERRY *and* ORANGE JELLIES

Though perhaps more reminiscent of a children's party than the grandeur of a cold banqueting table, this classic fine jelly recipe is fun as a party dessert and practical because it can be made up to 2 days in advance.

SERVES 15

INGREDIENTS

1 pint (600 ml) freshly squeezed
  orange juice, strained
1 teaspoon freshly squeezed
  lemon juice, strained
2 oz (50 g) powdered gelatine
1 pint (600 ml) water
1 tablespoon dry white wine
11 oz (300 g) sugar
2 tablespoons Grand Marnier
30 ice cubes, crushed into a
  polythene bag
8 oz (225 g) fresh raspberries
4 small tangerines or satsumas,
  unpeeled, cut into thin slices
icing sugar for dusting

1. Mix together the orange juice and lemon juice. Put the wine into a saucepan with the sugar, and add one third of the fruit juice. Sprinkle the gelatine over the liquid and leave it to be absorbed. This will take about 3 minutes. Place the saucepan over a low heat and warm the liquid through for 5 minutes, then remove from the heat and stir in the remaining fruit juice and the Grand Marnier.

2. Pour the liquid into a glass bowl. Put the crushed ice into a larger bowl and stand the glass bowl in this while the liquid cools, stirring at regular intervals. Pour the jelly into 25–30 small fluted tartlet moulds and place in the refrigerator.

3. After about an hour, remove the moulds from the refrigerator and place a single raspberry into each mould. The liquid should be viscous enough for the raspberry to be submerged yet suspended. Replace the moulds in the refrigerator and chill for a further 2 hours, until completely set.

4. When you are ready to serve the jellies, stand the moulds in a baking tray and fill it to the brim of the moulds with hot water. The water needs to be this high so that the jelly is loosened all over. Leave to stand for 1 minute. Place a slice of tangerine over the base of each mould, invert and turn out the jelly on to the tangerine slice. Serve on a tray dusted with icing sugar.

SWEET CRISPY BEAN CURD

INGREDIENTS
4 cakes bean curd, each about
2¼–2½ inches (6–6.5 cm) square,
drained
vegetable oil for deep-frying
4 tablespoons cornflour
1 tablespoon caster sugar
caster sugar for dipping

Besides the firm cakes of bean curd, the Chinese also make a soft, junket-like bean curd which is served warm or cold in a bowl, sweetened with a sugar syrup. Thought-association has prompted me to devise this sweet crispy bean curd, to be served hot with drinks.

SERVES 8–10

1. Quarter each cake of bean curd, then halve each piece widthways, making 32 cubes all together. Stand them on two or three layers of kitchen paper to absorb some of the excess moisture.

2. Half fill a wok or deep-fryer with oil and heat over a high heat until the oil reaches 375°F (190°C).

3. In the meantime, put the cornflour in a dish, add the sugar and mix thoroughly. Dip the bean curd, piece by piece, into the cornflour, turning it so that all the surfaces are covered. Discard the leftover cornflour.

4. With wooden tongs or chopsticks, carefully place half the pieces of bean curd in the oil and deep-fry for 2 minutes, until the skin is crisp but the inside still soft and curd-like. Gently move the bean curd around in the oil, separating any pieces that may have stuck together, about halfway through the time. Because of the sugar in the cornflour, part of the skin may turn golden brown quite quickly. Remove the bean curd from the oil using a large perforated hand strainer or slotted spoon, and stand the pieces on kitchen paper to absorb excess oil.

5. Place a saucer of caster sugar in the centre of a large serving plate and arrange the pieces of bean curd around it. Serve hot, and let your guests use their fingers to pick up the pieces and dip them into the sugar for added sweetness.

Note: Even though it is not advisable to prepare the crispy bean curd in advance, pieces that have become cold and limp can nevertheless be recrisped in a 350°F (180°C) gas mark 4 oven for 5–7 minutes.

Sweet Cashew Nuts

These cashew nuts, with their undertone of sweetness, are very alluring. They are a fitting item to add to a repertoire of five or six savoury eats for a party.

SERVES 12–15

INGREDIENTS
1 lb (450 g) shelled cashew nuts
¾ pint (450 ml) cold water
8 oz (225 g) sugar
vegetable oil for deep-frying
2 teaspoons toasted white sesame
   seeds

1. Blanch the nuts in boiling water for about a minute, then drain in a colander.

2. Put the ¾ pint (450 ml) of water in a saucepan with the sugar and set over a low heat until the sugar is completely dissolved. Add the blanched nuts to the syrup and bring to the boil, then simmer over a medium heat for 5 minutes. Remove the pan from the heat and leave the nuts to soak in the syrup for 1–2 hours so that they will take on more of the sugar flavour.

3. Tip the nuts into a sieve and leave to drain for approximately 10 mins.

4. Heat the oil to 350°F (180°C) and transfer the nuts to the wok using a slotted spoon, thus reducing the amount of sugar syrup mixing with the hot oil. Deep fry the nuts for 2–3 minutes until they take on a golden brown colour.

5. Remove the nuts from the oil using a large hand strainer or slotted spoon, and place them in a dish lined with greaseproof paper. Sprinkle the sesame seeds over the nuts and immediately move them around in the dish to ensure an even coating. Serve at room temperature.

Note: If stored in an airtight container, the nuts will keep for up to a fortnight.

INDEX